THE WORLD'S MOST FAMOUS BUS DRIVER

By
Tommy Steele

FINIAL PUBLISHING

Published February 2001
FINIAL PUBLISHING

ISBN 1-900467-09-X

Produced by Finial Publishing & Printing Services
15 Hoburne Road, Swanage, Dorset BH19 2SL, England
Telephone/Fax: 01929 423980
Email: mail@finial.co.uk

Printed by The Dorset Press, Dorchester, Dorset DT1 1HD

DEDICATION

I would like to dedicate this book to my father
Tommy Steele
for making a soapbox on wheels for me
and to my mother
May Christina Steele
for her gentle manner, which taught me that
anger is a wasted emotion.

Last stop for Tommy Steele

By Paula Roberts

TOMMY Steele – just like his famous namesake – has been singing to audiences for more than two decades.

But unlike the top entertainer he hasn't been performing to huge crowds at the London Palladium.

For this Tommy Steele is Dorset's one and only singing bus driver and while he has been driving he has been serenading his passengers.

Now he's decided to hang up his ticket machine after 21 years and pick up a bus pass.

It hasn't been all plain sailing for the mobile crooner. Tommy, of Station Road, Parkstone, hit the headlines 12 years ago when he was gagged by bus bosses for blasting tuneful melodies on his routes around Bournemouth.

But when the Daily Echo spoke out on his behalf, Yellow Buses had a change of heart and told Tommy he could carry on. The

65-year-old granddad plans to write a book about his driving days.

He said: "My job driving coaches and buses was pure joy and over the years I collected many humorous stories."

To keep these stories alive Tommy speaks at after-dinner parties to small groups retelling the days of when he made all his early morning passengers sit and hold hands and

say "I love you" and "Good morning neighbour" to break the silence.

In his spare time he is a volunteer worker at the Swanage Steam Railway booking office.

Tommy once tried his hand at being a traffic warden but after working for three different coach companies his real love was bus driving. "I am a lucky man. I always enjoyed work and people," he said.

At one point he was juggling bus driving with being a DJ for hospital broadcasting service Radio Bedside.

"I was put on this earth to make people laugh. I think I succeeded about 75 per cent," he added.

Top Five songs for swinging bus-kers

1	............................Ticket to Ride
2	...............................Day Tripper
3	....................................Bus Stop
4	................My Ting-Ting-a-Ling
5	....I'm Still Standing

(or anything by Desmond Double-Dekker)

ALL WRITE NOW: Driver Tommy Steele is writing his memoirs

Picture: Hattie Miles

From the *Daily Echo* (Bournemouth), Friday June 4, 1999. Courtesy, News Communications & Media PLC

CONTENTS

INTRODUCTION

Why write books about being on the buses? I said books, because when I started my training as a conductor some nine years ago, a member of staff said I should write a book about the job, as nobody really knows what it is like to drive a bus. So, I started a card index of stories – both humorous and sad – of my experiences as a conductor, crew bus driver, then a one-person bus driver and coach driver. As the number of entries in my index increased, I began to realise that instead of a single book, I had enough material for an *omnibus*.

As I write this, in front of me is a copy of the Bournemouth *Daily Echo* of Thursday 10 August 2000. One headline reads, 'Wilts & Dorset cannot run a full service because of a shortage of bus drivers, despite offering over £6 per hour!'. Why? Turn to the 'Letters' columns of the same newspaper and you will read 'Bus Ride to Hell!', describing a late night terror ride by a passenger with a gang of drunken yobs, smoking, swearing, jumping up and down and ringing the bell, the poor old driver having to contend with all this while driving. A passenger contacted Yellow Buses and was informed, 'It's the same every night on the last buses. No-one wants to work on them and everyone is frightened'.

Let me take you dear readers back to the FUN days of bus driving!

TOMMY STEELE
February 2001

ACKNOWLEDGEMENTS

In writing this book, I would like to thank first of all my publishers – David Clifford and John Villers - of Finial Publishing, Swanage, because without their help this book would never have been published. Thanks also to Andrew P M Wright for the zany photograph of me, used at the start of each chapter.

Secondly, you cannot write a book without a pen, so a few years back Audrey bought me a superb Sheaffer pen and said, "Get writing!". Incidentally, this pen still has the original cartridge, so many thanks to the Sheaffer Pen Company, whose excellent product has made writing this book so much easier.

The Managing Director of Yellow Buses, Bournemouth – Mr. R. E. Edgley – who kindly gave permission to include maps, timetables and other Yellow Bus material.

My sincere thanks to Neal Butterworth (Editor) and Ed Perkins (Deputy Editor) for permission to use material published in the *Daily Echo*.

I would also like to thank the numerous reporters who have interviewed me and wrote about all the humorous incidents I have been involved in over the years: Radio Solent and 2CR, BBC Radio 2 and TV South Today, Meridian TV; Newspapers – *Star*, *Sun* and *Daily Mirror* and Hospital Radio.

Last, but not least, my wonderful bus mates and *you* – the passengers – for providing me with so many funny stories.

TOMMY STEELE
February 2001

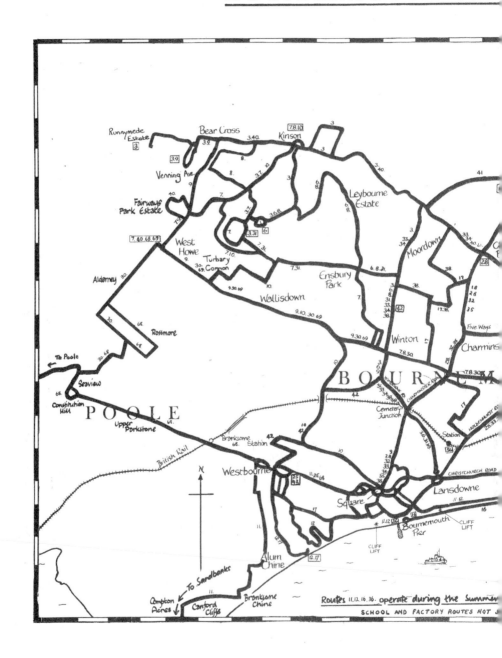

Routes 11.12.16.36. operate during the Summer
SCHOOL AND FACTORY ROUTES NOT

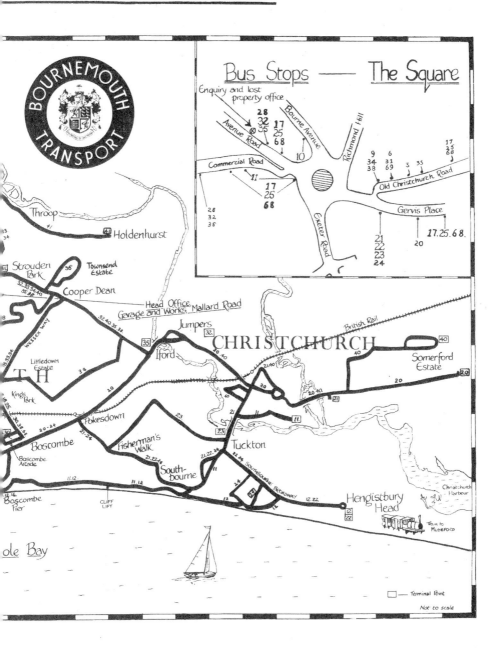

TOMMY'S TICKLERS!

Two drunks late at night outside a bus depot. One turns to the other and says, "Let's nick a bus, to save walking home". "OK. I'll nip in and get one." He comes back 10 minutes later, "It's no good. We'll have to walk. I can't find a Number 6 bus in there".

"Well, you could have nicked a Number 3, which would have taken us to Cemetery Junction and we could have walked from there."

Two old ladies, late at night, approach the Inspector in the Bus station. One says, "Excuse me, Inspector, has the last Number 6 gone?".

"Yes Madam."

"And has the last Number 10 gone?"

"Yes Madam."

"And what about the last Number 8, has that gone as well?"

"Madam. All the buses have gone."

"Thank goodness for that! Come on, Ethel. It's safe to cross the bus station now."

A man gets on a one-man operated bus, looking very ill.

"Where to?", asks the driver.

"Cemetery."

"Single or return?"

"Single. I'm not coming back."

"Oh dear! Sorry to here that", said the driver.

BUS DRIVER? DON'T MAKE ME LAUGH!

Since the age of about nine, buses have fascinated me, my earliest memories are going to school on a service London Transport bus, with an open staircase at the back to climb up to the upper saloon (for bus enthusiasts, this was an ST). In those days, school special buses were not even thought of; you had to walk to school, or cycle in my case, although sometimes, my mother, if she had some shopping to do, would take me in a pushchair. This was alright, but the other children would laugh at me (mind you, I was sixteen!).

This experience also enabled me to discover the secret of how to go through life when people are making fun of you – just laugh with them. They like to think they have scored and it's very disconcerting to the person making fun at someone else's misfortune, to find that person laughing with them. Also, if you are going to make a joke about a person, make it against yourself. That way, people are not laughing *at* you, but *with* you.

Similarly, the way to win an argument, is not to argue if a person tries to argue with you – you do not reply. He (or she), I say 'she' because most of us have wives, are left with their own words. Oh! How I thank my mother for teaching me the ground rules of life, rules which helped me through life, especially working on the buses.

In all my times on buses and coaches (twenty-three years), I could count on two fingers the number of arguments I have been involved in and on both occasions, the person apologized. Ignoring my advice never to let the other person's attitude effect yours, many of my mates got involved in several arguments every day.

There was one driver, called Don and I would say, "Morning Don, alright?".

"I'm alright until I get out there and a passenger upsets me."

"What a lovely way to start the day", I would say, then I would start singing, 'All things bright and beautiful'.

"Don't start, I'm not in the mood."

"You married, Don?"

"I was, but my wife ran off."

"Oh! I'm not surprised. Perhaps, you'll meet some other lucky woman?"

At this, Don brightened up, but added that if I was his conductor, "I don't want no singing, while you're working with me, alright?". This I found hard to do and we would often end up, when we had our meal-break in the canteen, with him sitting at another table, moaning about me.

I've written these words to give you, dear reader, some reasons why if you are inclined to be argumentative and cannot laugh at life, you should think twice about working on the buses. A lot of busmen (and some women) would be better off not working with the public, but instead working in a factory, or similar, although it's strange these people work for years in bus work, unconcerned with the arguments they have with passengers and their mates. Me, I've enjoyed every minute of a job, where no two days were the same.

Although I'm running ahead of my early days, I am setting the scene, so back to my early love of buses. During my school days, I lived at Southall, in Middlesex. My father, a stand-up comedian, often used the joke, that I was an only child, without brothers and sisters: "I wanted a boy, my wife wanted a girl – with him, *we got both*". Early days of learning to laugh at myself!

One day, my love of riding on buses almost cost me my life. Coming home from school one afternoon, with my friend Derek Russell, we overrode our bus stop at Park Avenue, ending up at Southall Bus Garage. At that time of the day, not many buses were on garage, so we decided to have a good look around. I've always been a bit of a daredevil, so I climbed up into the cab of an STL.

But, the thrill of sitting behind the wheel of a double-decker bus, imagining I was driving down the Uxbridge Road, was cut short. A shout of, "Oy! What are you doing in that cab?", shattered my dreams, particularly when I found the Garage foreman advancing with rapid pace in my direction. My rapid pace was even quicker, falling out of the half-cab onto the floor and dodging a swipe aimed at my ear – in those days, you received instant justice – a cuff round the ear! (goodness knows today what a cuff round the ear would be worth in the Court of Human Rights?).

In my younger days, I had a good turn of speed and I somehow managed to elude the foreman's attentions, eventually joining Derek – both breathless – on the pavement outside the Garage. As we walked back towards the huge iron bridge which carried the Great Western Railway main lines to and from Paddington, we saw the familiar sign high-up on the bridge, 'A.E.C. Motor Vehicles Diesel Engines Factory Service & Spares Depot', with an arrow pointing to 'paradise', namely the site where London's buses were built, as well as buses for services all over Great Britain and, indeed, overseas.

"Tell you what", said Derek, "Let's take a short cut home and cross over the bridge." This, indeed, would be a short cut home, as Park Avenue, where we lived, backed onto the railway line. Even in those days, what we were about to do, was extremely foolhardy and dangerous, but we were young and didn't see the danger we were placing ourselves in. Climbing the embankment, we walked onto the bridge itself and when we were about half way across, I stopped, looking down at the road below which served the A.E.C. Works. At that moment, a brand-spanking-new, shiny-red-liveried RT London Transport bus came out of the Works and I stood mesmerized, just imagining that I was at the wheel.

I was so engrossed, that I failed to hear Derek's shout, "*Look out!*", nor to realize that I was standing almost on the main line. With that, Derek grabbed my arm and threw me forward, just as a GWR 'King' class locomotive thundered by, whistling shrilly, with about 12 coaches behind. Quickly, we made our way back down the embankment to the safety of the road and I thanked Derek for saving my life. The irony of this story, is that I was born one Sunday afternoon, in a house at Scotts Road, which backed onto the Great Western Railway. If I had had been killed, it would have been within a mile of where I was born and if Derek Russell ever reads this book, I would like him to get in touch with me, as I owe him a dinner.

Schooldays were spent travelling round on London Transport buses, which were all 'half-cabs' in those days (for the bus enthusiast, 'half-cabs' had the engine at the front and the driver sat in his cab next to it). During my bus service, I was to come across many of the older drivers, who still longed for the old days, when they had been isolated from the public, being shut inside their cabs, modern buses, of course, having the driver sitting inside the bus itself. However, I'm not sure that I could have stood bells ringing in my ears all day: one ring to stop; two to go and three, full right up.

I always used to travel in the front seat behind the driver, so that I could watch him driving the bus and I think that it was in those days, that I first got the desire to become a bus driver. I used to think that all buses were named 'Donald Duck', until one day, when I looked more closely and found the words were 'double deck'! This was written clearly above the driver's head in the cab of the bus and was a reminder to him in case of any low bridges that he might encounter.

To this day, my favourite colour for a bus is red and it almost made me feel glad to be waiting at a bus stop on a dark, winter night and see a well-lit red bus coming towards me. During my courting days, I made a habit of catching (just), the last 65 bus from Richmond Ice Rink, to Brentford, then seeing the last 655 trolley bus come round from Griffin Park (Brentford Football Club's Ground). To take me to Hanwell, I had to walk to Southall, because the last 607 (Shepherds Bush to Uxbridge) had long gone. Happy days! Not many cars on the road; no road rage and more buses.

There were a variety of sorts of buses to choose from in those days, including the old Guy 'Arab' (with wooden seats), just the job for school specials! I suppose you could say my first impression of buses was sitting on wooden seats. Ian Allan (who would later become the biggest publisher of transport books in this country), brought out in 1948, a small book which sold for two shillings – 'The ABC of London Transport. No. 1 – Buses and Coaches' and book in hand, bus spotting became my favourite hobby.

Hanging around Hanwell and Putney Garages, spotting 'STLs', 'STLTs', 'RTs' and a real 'cop' (term used to spot a rare bus in that area), an 'Interstation C' bus, which was a coach, but half way along the roof, it had a top deck. By this time, I had made friends with the foreman at Southall Bus Garage. Sometimes he would give me a tour and one day he even let me climb into a bus cab and sit behind the steering wheel in the cab. That was what decided me. 'That's it!', I thought to myself, 'I will be become a bus driver one day'.

I used to watch the bus crews changing over outside Southall Garage and it enthralled me to watch the driver climb up to his driving cab, slide the door open, get in and then pull away. The bus would disappear into the distance with a roar from the A.E.C. diesel engine and a cloud of diesel smoke from where it had been left ticking over (I can still hear in my head, this sound to this day).

My father worked at A.E.C. as a skilled engineer (he never made enough money as a comedian) and he suggested that on leaving school, I go to work in the offices at A.E.C., as he did not want me to work in the oil and filth of a factory. I can remember going to my first interview and walking through the tunnel which carried the Great Western Railway (now Railtrack) railway lines to and from Paddington. We were a poor family, but my late mother was very good at patching and mending clothes. My one and only pair of shoes, had large holes in the soles (sounds a bit like a title for a pop song!) and my mother had filled the holes with cardboard for me. I remember walking through the rain on my way to the interview for the post of junior office boy, in my patched clothes and despite my mother's best efforts, my feet were soon soaking wet, the cardboard acting like blotting paper.

By the time I had reached the A.E.C. Works, the cardboard had completely disintegrated, leaving my patched socks soaking wet and I might as well have been walking in bare feet! Anyway, the people at A.E.C. did not notice my shoes and offered me a job in their Progress Department. People today have no real idea what it was like to be poor, that's why I have dedicated this book to my parents.

You could say I made progress (to coin a pun) and after office training, you went out into the Works and located batches of parts needed for the engine assembly plant, that they were short of, a big problem in those days. Parts to keep London Transport buses on the road, were often delayed around the factory, so it was my job to round them up. The person in charge, told me that I had a job for life, instead it seemed that I was serving life! Anyway, he was wrong. A.E.C. closed its doors for the last time on 25th May 1979 and now A.E.C. buses can only be found in museum collections. In those days, it would not have seemed possible that such a vast Works, with order books full for years ahead, would close.

I became bored with the job, but not with the buses. The outside yard was filled with fully-fitted-out buses ex-body works, which then had to come back to the main Works for final testing. The sight of a 'Regent' or 'Renown' model in the livery and paintwork of the corporation they were destined for, stirred my blood and one day, I knew *I was going to drive one of those buses.*

On occasions, I managed to have a look inside one of the new buses and the smell of the real leather seats was a heady perfume. In those days, buses could run round in service, without the mindless slashing and defacing of seats we have today by some of our mindless members of society.

During the 1950s, this country had conscription (National Service), where young men were called into the Armed Forces. I was one of these and two years later, I left the Army, but my life had changed. I was not going back to work in a factory, so I took a job in a furniture shop and found that I had the 'gift of the gab' selling furniture.

After getting married and finding myself with two daughters – and short of money having moved to Bournemouth – I became a part-time stand-up comedian. This had started after doing an audition for Television South, in St. Peter's Hall, Bournemouth. I didn't make any progress on TV, but I got myself a comedy routine (gags mostly stolen from other comedians) and tried my act round the pubs and clubs, or to anybody who would listen.

It looks easy on TV telling jokes, with the audience primed to laugh in the studio, but try telling jokes in a noisy club or pub (I still have the mental scars of trying a 'clean' routine with the sailors of Portsmouth – my act lasted all of two minutes!). My comedy routines always went better with the people I worked with - perhaps, it was because they didn't have to pay?

I suppose my furniture days and my act, both came to an abrupt end in a large Bournemouth department store. With the manager away, I gave the staff in the Soft Furnishing Department a 'soft shoe shuffle'. The act (for a change) was going so well, that I failed to notice the managing director walk into the department. I wondered why my colleagues suddenly seemed to lose interest in my dancing. Me, I continued my act at the Labour Exchange next day!

The only job I could get was selling insurance on a commission-only basis and looking back over the years, I recall becoming area 'Salesman of the Year', then sales instructor and finally team manager. The job entailed working mostly seven days a week, but it was my paperwork, which let me down. I can sell till the cows come home, but paperwork is not my scene. I'm a salesman, pure and simple, not a manager of men who are all on a commission–only basis. My performance suffered, until I was forced to go off sick with depression.

One of my favourite sayings is, 'In life we sometimes have to go through a bad period to get to a good period' and for me this certainly proved the case. One day, sitting at home, feeling sorry for myself, I thought back to the soapbox on wheels that my father had made for me (more about this in the next chapter) and my dream of becoming a bus driver. There and then, I decided, 'That's it! I'm going to be a bus driver!'. My friends tried their best to talk me out of it, bus driving being considered in our class-conscious society, a demeaning job – far from it!

Being a one-man bus driver, in my opinion, is far harder that flying an aeroplane. Think about it? During my time, I have often had to stand up and introduce myself to groups of people and I was always proud to say that I was a bus driver. Little did I know that being a bus driver would make me famous - thanks to the Bournemouth *Evening Echo* - after being banned from singing on my bus. This led to interviews on TV and Radio 2 and coverage in newspapers and magazines worldwide; my own show on Radio Bedside; open fetes; compère fashion shows and place me on the panel of the Independent Broadcasting Authority (IBA), monitoring the broadcasting output of our local radio station 2CR. In addition, the *Evening Echo* gave me a News Years Honour and after speaking to the audience after the Mayor of Bournemouth's presentation, I was encouraged to become a public speaker.

Twenty-three happy years later, few people would wish that they had spent more time at the office - I do. However, the nice thing about writing an autobiography about a job you love, is that you live it all over again; the marvellous characters I worked with and most of all, *you* the passengers. Somebody once said, buses are the only place where the customers are the enemy. Don't believe it, anyway not on my bus! You all kept me entertained so much, that since I started in 1978, I have written all the funny stories down and in this first book you will find some of them (more to come in future books).

This time, they are for your entertainment.

SETTING THE SCENE

About the age of nine, my father had made me a soapbox on wheels. Some readers will not know what this is, so let me explain.

Just after the Second World War, soap was delivered to shops in wooden boxes, which were useful for all kinds of purposes. My father obtained one such box from a local shop and I watched enthralled as he cut the front away, leaving two sides and a back. This three-sided box would form the seat and this was screwed on the top of a 4-ft long by 1-ft wide plank of wood. Four old pram wheels were found from somewhere and secured onto the two metal bars which formed the axles. As my father was an engineer, it was easy enough for him to secure the two axles to the underneath of the plank, the rear one fixed, the front swivelling on a bolt. Attached to each side of the front axles, was a rope long enough to reach back to where I was sat, these 'reins' enabling me to steer. *There were no brakes!*

We lived on top of a short, steep hill and I would fearlessly climb into the soapbox and hurtle to the bottom. There were few cars or other traffic in those days and if any one was crossing the road, I would shout "Look out!". This was usually followed by a cry of "Young hooligan!" and I would glimpse a fist being shaken in my direction as I shot past. On reaching the bottom of the hill, I would haul my soapbox back to the top and start all over again. I did this for years, from dawn to dusk and it was my first taste of driving - I loved it.

I told all my school friends, some day I was going to drive a big red bus and many a time when I have been driving my bus, I think back to the times of my soapbox days and the skill of my father, for the soapbox lasted many years, despite some harsh treatment.

True to my word, my career on the road started in 1979 with Yellow Buses, after spotting an advertisement in the then *Evening Echo* for bus conductors. Good rates of pay and holidays, etc were on offer, but the part that caught my eye, was that conductors could apply to be trained as bus drivers after six months.

After filling in various forms, I presented myself for an interview at Mallard Road, Bournemouth, the main bus depot for the then Bournemouth Transport. The interviewer, having heard my jokes to his question, "Why had I applied?", such as "I thought the advert for conductors was for the Bournemouth Symphony Orchestra", or "I want to tell people where to get off", was intrigued and said, "Mr. Steel. You are a successful sales manager, earning more in one week, than a conductor's wages for a month".

I replied, "I've wanted to drive a bus ever since living in London years ago and driving an RT bus with a driving instructor for a trial run from Hounslow Garage on a Sunday morning". At the time, London Transport were so short of drivers, that they were offering anybody with a clean car driving licence, a chance to try a drive to see if they would like the job. After my run, the instructor said, that "After training, You will make a good driver".

The interviewer then informed me, that after I had passed a medical, I would be offered the job, with a view of driver training, after a period of conducting.

I next found myself in Boscombe, sitting in the waiting room of the bus company doctor, surrounded by hundreds of classical records. The doctor came in and called each applicant's name in turn. Sitting next to me, one chap called out, "Got any Adam and the Ants records, doctor?". I passed my medical and I don't think that anyone ever failed. The bus companies were so short of staff, that even if you had one leg, you were in!

On a dull Monday morning, I presented myself to the Training School at Mallard Road Bus Depot, which consisted of a gloomy room with pictures of trams and buses around the walls. One picture stuck in my mind, as it showed a bus smashed into a wall, with the caption 'THE DRIVER OF THIS BUS WAS KILLED!'. I heard the person standing next to me, say "I'm sticking to conducting".

In the room were five other would-be conductors, although after two days the number reduced to four, as one person found, as he put it, that "I cannot stand heights". This was after going upstairs on a double-decker bus in the Depot on the third day of training. We also lost another would-be conductor after he came back from being taken around all the routes on an empty bus – he suffered from bus sickness!

Sharply at nine o'clock one morning, Inspector Dennis Buxton entered the room. He said "Good morning lads" and then promptly counted heads – six should have been eight! At 10–past–nine, applicant number seven turned up, "Sorry I'm late – I overslept". He was dismissed, with the words "If you can't get up in the morning, you're no good to us – the passengers won't wait for you".

Inspector Buxton's opening address has always remained in my mind, "Bus work is a wonderful job to the right person, who wants to do it. To the wrong person, its crucifixion". During my career, I found most of my workmates suffered crucifixion every day!

Our last day before going 'on the road' was spent looking around the Mallard Road Depot. Bournemouth Transport at that time, had 120 buses, made up of Leyland Atlanteans and Leyland Fleetlines double-deckers, most of which would be in-service during the rush hour. Up to six buses at a time could be serviced at any one time and the reason why bus travel is so safe, is that they are serviced regularly. Normally, one or two buses would be kept in reserve, to cover breakdowns.

One of the least known jobs – and the dirtiest – was steam cleaning the underside of the vehicle. The procedure was that the bus would be hoisted up onto a ramp and a mechanic in a hard-hat and waterproof, protective clothing worked underneath with a high-pressure hose, blasting off the dirt, oil and grease.

The Upholstery Shop at the Depot had an amazing collection of bus seats, many slashed and defaced and it is, perhaps, a little disturbing that some people cannot travel on a bus without defacing a seat.

One of the funniest stories I heard, concerned a seat. One of the drivers, who was a bit of a ladies' man, played around with a married lady passenger, then dropped her. To get revenge, the lady wrote all the intimate details about the driver's love-making, plus the size of his manhood and his name in large letters on the seat of a bus. The seat was, of course, removed from the vehicle and the seat left outside the Inspector's Office for everybody to read. Concerning the remarks on his manhood, his leg was pulled in the canteen with comments such as "Barry was offered a part in the nude musical Hair. It was ideal for him as it was only a *small part!*".

Last of all, Inspector Buxton drove us round all the routes and explained the use of the emergency doors on the bus. Tomorrow, we would be out on the road with different, more experienced conductors keeping an eye on us for a few days. However, although we should have been working *with* them, I found myself working *for* them.

TOMMY'S TICKLERS!

Conductor goes upstairs to collect a Scotsman's fare. The passenger is wearing full Highland dress, right down to a kilt.

The Scotsman offers his fare to the conductor, who says, "That will be 50 pence for you and 25 pence for your dog".

"I have na dog!"

"Yes, you have. It's laying on your kilt."

"That's a sporran."

With that, the lady sitting next to the Scotsman faints. When she comes round, she gasps, "To think, I've been stroking it since Bournemouth!".

A Scotsman gets off the bus and drops a bottle of whisky on the pavement, which smashes. With that, he starts crying.

"Never mind", says the conductor, "You can always buy another one".

"It's nay that. I've lost all my luggage and I'm on holiday, mon!"

BACK IN
THE CLASSROOM

Back in the classroom, Inspector Buxton outlined the Company and the job. In 1979, the name of the bus company was Bournemouth Transport and their buses were painted in blue and yellow livery and ever since I can remember, the public has known and called the local buses 'Yellows'. Later, the Company changed its image and adopted a new livery of brown and yellow. The name 'YELLOW BUSES' along the side of the vehicle was in brown, as were the rims of the wheels. The company logo on the sides of the bus was also changed at the same time, to that of a round wheel in blue.

More recently, the livery has reverted back to blue and yellow, but without the round wheel logo on the side. In addition, the General Manager's name is printed in small black letters by the door and thanks to this, the Company does not change its GM too often, as this would mean 120 buses having to be altered each time a change took place!

Inspector Buxton, in outlining the Company and the job, told us that Bournemouth Transport covered the area from Westbourne, down to Somerford, Castle Lane, Throop, Charminster, Moordown, Kinson, Bear Cross, Wallisdown and that outside that area, was Wilts & Dorset territory. In those days, Bournemouth Transport did not operate to Poole - that would come later with the No. 30 service one-man operation. However, some Wilts & Dorset buses did operate to Bournemouth Square, both companies having a gentleman's agreement not to run over each other's area, as this would only trigger off a bus war, which in the end both companies would lose by being forced to cut fares.

This was to prove an accurate prediction, because later, when another company tried to take over in Bournemouth by cutting fares and bringing back conductors, the public at first loved the war, but in the end stayed with the Yellows. This cost the other bus company the war and didn't help the bus drivers much. When new Yellow drivers were taken on, this was on a reduced hourly rate, compared with the regular Yellow bus drivers.

Bournemouth Square played a major part in our area of operations and when I first started work on the buses, the Inspectors used to control operations from a small wooden hut at the bottom of Avenue Road, opposite Woolworths (now Boots Chemists). Later, the Inspectors had an office built over the toilets in Avenue Road ("very apt", said one wag!). Buses used to be parked in Avenue Road and also Bournemouth Triangle, which sometimes a dozy driver (me), not reading his duty sheet ie when commencing a duty, would take a bus from the wrong place and in the process, upset the running order and the Inspectors! It was at this location that some older readers may well remember a very bad tram crash, when on the evening of 1st May 1908, a new tram careered out of control and shot off the rails at a bend in Avenue Road. It plunged down a steep and heavily-wooded slope into a private garden. Seven people were killed and many seriously injured, in what was to become one of the worst electric tram disasters in this country.

The Mallard Road main bus depot, works, offices and garage (now a listed building), was also a signing-on point for duty crews. Similarly, the Inspector's hut in the Square was also a signing-on point. Mallard Road was mainly used in the mornings, all the buses leaving from here. The Square was only used for late duty signing-on. One of the problems experienced by bus crews signing-on at Mallard Road in the morning, was that if your duty turn finished in the Square, you then had to get a bus back to Mallard Road to collect your car, thus adding about thirty minutes (unpaid) onto your day's work. Conductors and drivers had to sign *on*, but not *off*!

Having explained the signing-on procedure, Inspector Buxton went on to explain our duties. These consisted of early turn, middle turn ('spread over') and late turn. I will explain:

Early turn could start as early as 5.30 a.m. and last for eight hours (with a meal break) and finish (depending on start time) up to 3.30 p.m. Staff who could get up in the morning, enjoyed it when one conductor, who found it difficult to get up, came into sign-on and the Inspector said "Late again?".

"First time this year, Inspector."

"I know. But it's only the 1st January!"

Middle turn signing-on in the Square, was mainly from 9 a.m. onwards, lasting until 5 p.m., with a meal break. This was not a popular turn if your duty finished at Mallard Road, when the bus ran empty back to the garage.

'Spread Over' could start from 7 a.m. onwards (to cover the rush hour) and finish after three hours. You could then go home, come back again from 2 p.m. and work up to 7 p.m. The nice thing about 'Spread Over', apart from your meal break, was that you were paid for the whole duty, so you could go home, dig the garden or lay on the beach and still be paid. However, a lot of people thought it was too-long-a-day.

Late turns started from 3.30 p.m. onwards and could finish between 10 p.m. and midnight. The most popular sort – after late turn – was a 'straight through', so-called because you started from 5 p.m. and worked with only a short break, finishing at 11 p.m. onwards.

You were allowed to change your duty with another conductor, providing you informed the Traffic Office. 'Straight Throughs' were easy to swap, because some men had another job in the day. One such, was a painter and decorator, who always looked tired.

After passing your test to become a driver, you could always swap an early conducting turn (they were called 'turns' instead of duties) for a late driving turn. Mind you, it had to be a good early turn ie one that started and finished early. If you did this on a regular basis, you were called 'Wheel Happy'! I could not get enough driving and my nickname was 'Wheel-e Happy'. One of my less complementary nicknames was 'Shot Away', because I enjoyed the job so much, although my mates in the canteen regarded me with some suspicion.

Inspector Buxton then explained the rota system, which was worked by seniority. It went like this:

'Spare Conductors' Rota', which meant that you did not find out which duty you were on for the following week, until the previous Friday. When the Traffic Office put up the duty sheets for the following week, you could find yourself on a late turn, which made planning ahead for theatre visits etc difficult. The Traffic Office would not change your duty. You had to find somebody willing to change, which meant finding somebody to work a late turn on a Saturday night – difficult!

Then came 'Conductor Rota', which meant you could plan ahead for a few weeks. After passing your test, you started all over again on the 'Spare Drivers' Rota'. A few conductors stayed as conductors all their working lives, because they may not have wanted to drive and some were unable to drive for medical reasons.

There was another rota called the 'Rush Conductors'. These were men who had worked for years, both as conductors and drivers, who were kept in the Garage as 'standby', in case somebody rang in sick at the last moment. This was not a bad job, as most of your time could be spent sitting around reading the paper, waiting for something to happen.

Inspector Buxton had told us that "This job runs on tea or two Ts – tea and toilets!", although I found this not to be true. The job ran on endless memos from the Traffic Office, asking for an explanation as to why you did a certain thing, or why you didn't do a certain thing? If your reply was not convincing, it was followed by a visit to the Office for an interview with the Traffic Manager, where you had to explain yourself.

BOURNEMOUTH TRANSPORT

FARE SCALES

Scale 'A' - to apply to ordinary bus services, except Services 11 and 12

No. of Stages	Approx. Mileage	Adult Fare	Child and Dog
1	0.45	7p	5p
2	0.90	9p	6p
3	1.35	11p	7p
4	1.80	14p	8p
5	2.25	16p	9p
6/7	3.15	18p	11p
8-12	5.40	21p	12p
over 12	over 5.40	24p	12p

Scale 'B' - to apply to Summer Pleasure Services 11 and 12

No. of Stages	Approx. Mileage	Adult Fare	Child and Dog
1	0.80	10p	6p
2	1.60	15p	9p
3	2.40	20p	12p
4	3.20	25p	15p
5	4.00	25p	15p
6	4.80	30p	20p
7	5.60	30p	20p
8	6.40	35p	20p
9	7.20	35p	20p
10	8.00	40p	25p
11	8.70	40p	25p
12	9.10	45p	30p
13	9.50	45p	30p
14	9.90	50p	30p
15	10.30	50p	30p
16	10.70	50p	30p
17	11.10	55p	30p
18	11.50	55p	30p

(Cover shown at left:) BOURNEMOUTH TRANSPORT — **FARES** — COMMENCING SUNDAY 21ST JANUARY

21	BOURNEMOUTH SQUARE - CHRISTCHURCH	21
22	BOURNEMOUTH SQUARE - HENGISTBURY HEAD	22

	Adult	Child
	7	5
	9	6
	11	7
	14	8
	16	9
	18	11
	21	12
	24	12

```
            SQUARE (4)
         7  Wootton Gardens or St. Peter's Road (5)
         9  7  Lansdowne (6)
        11  9  7  Derby Road (7)
        14 11  9  7  Boscombe Gardens (8)
        16 14 11  9  7  Boscombe Arcade (9)
        18 16 14 11  9  7  Parkwood Road (10)
        18 18 16 14 11  9  7  Pokesdown Rail Station (11)
        21 18 18 16 14 11  9  7  Fisherman's Walk (12)
        21 21 18 18 16 14 11  9  7  Tuckton Corner (13)
        21 21 21 18 18 16 14 11  9  7  Southbourne X.roads (14)
        21 21 21 21 18 18 16 14 11  9  7  TUCKTON BRIDGE (15)
        21 21 21 21 21 18 18 16 14 11  9  7  Barrack Road (Serv.21) or Saxon King Hotel (Ser.22) (16)
        24 21 21 21 21 21 18 18 16 14 11  9  7  X.church Town Hall (Ser.21) or HENG.HEAD (Ser.22) (17)
        24 24 21 21 21 21 21 18 18 16 14 11  9  7  BRIDGE STREET (18)
```

14

There was a 'merit' bonus, with so much put aside every week for 'good behaviour!'. After six months, the bonus was paid in a lump sum, less any deductions. For example, an Inspector could report a driver for running early and ahead of the timetable. If proved guilty, you received a memo informing you that two weeks' merit bonus would be deducted. These memos always ended with the comment 'You can appeal to your Union'. I once wrote on the back of memo, 'I do not appeal to them either!'. Mind you, the Traffic Office eventually got used to me. I once went to bed and had a dream. I was working overtime next morning and put in an overtime sheet!

We used to have sheets for 'Uncollected Fares' which had to be completed by the conductor and signed by the passenger. I was off duty travelling with my dog, when an Inspector boarded and I had to show him my pass.

"Have you paid for your dog?", he said.

I replied "He's got a Rover ticket".

He must have had a bad day and he was a bit like 'Blakey' from the TV series 'On the Buses' and he said "You will have to fill in an 'Uncollected Fare' form and send it in to the office with the fare".

One of the questions on the form asked 'Reason for non-payment?'. I wrote here 'Woof Woof Woof' and where the passenger was supposed to sign, I drew a paw mark and sent the form in. That story kept everybody amused for some time. Except the Inspector of course, who when boarding a bus, the crews went "Woof Woof"! and he did not appreciate jokes such as "What goes Woof-Tick-Woof?" Answer: A Watch Dog!

Back at the Training School, during our break in the canteen, we were approached by some union representatives - who were also busmen - and asked to join the Transport & General Workers' Union.

"What if I don't want to join?" said one of our party.

"It's a closed shop and you will not be here very long", he was informed.

"I will not be here long, *anyway*" and he didn't stay.

I would like to point out here, that at that time, there was plenty of five-day-a-week, well paid jobs with regular hours and with every weekend off available and the turnover of personnel was such that, you very quickly worked through the rotas to Driving School, then crew driver. *It took me six months.*

We spent two days in the classroom, being shown the fare charts and the ticket machines. These were very heavy and were called a 'Setright', so-called because all one had to do was set the dials and then just turn the handle. We were shown how to wear the machine around our necks and over our shoulders. Over the other shoulder, you had to wear a very heavy leather conductor's bag, which when new, the edges of the money compartments cut your fingers. Both were very heavy and cumbersome and with a full bag of silver and copper, the bag cut

15

into your shoulders and after running up and down stairs on a hot summer's day, you felt drained and looked like your passport photograph!

We also had to go through the Company Rule Book, make-up tickets and shown how to pay our money in, using a canvas bag placed in a safety deposit box.

There was a final word of warning from Inspector Buxton. He told us that a lot of people came onto the buses thinking they were going to make a fortune, by not issuing a ticket for a collected fare. He told us about one incident where a conductor on an open-top bus, when collecting the fares, wound off penny tickets, then as he gave the ticket to the passenger, let the ticket blow away in the wind. When an Inspector boarded the bus, the conductor would say he had issued a ticket and the passenger would confirm that the ticket had blown away. The Inspector then followed the bus in his own car, picking up the tickets. Faced with the evidence, the conductor was dismissed.

Inspector Buxton finally said, "One last thought. All our Inspectors started as conductors, then drivers, so they know all the tricks. Keep your nose clean and you have a job for life".

TOMMY'S TICKLERS!

Little boy sitting on his father's knee on a crowded bus. A gorgeous blonde gets on and stands holding the rail. The father turns to his son and says, "Come on, son. Give your seat up for the lady".

Driver bending over the open bonnet, looking at the engine, after the bus wouldn't start, turns to his clippie and says, "Get me a spanner, luv".
"Do you want a screw-driver as well?"
"Not now, luv, but wait until I get the bus started!

TRAINING ON THE ROAD

It's 7.30 in the morning at Mallard Road and after two days in the training school, I'm being allowed out on the road under the watchful eye of an experienced conductor. I'd been told that some of the conductors, when supervising, make you do all the work, while others give you a hand.

Bill, the Inspector who checked me in, was a big, bluff, kindly man, who had a pipe in his mouth permanently, or so it appeared. During all my years with the Yellows, I never saw him remove it once and it was rumoured that he was born with it!

He said, "You're on Bus 252 on Line 6". I should explain that the buses were all lined up in rows, ready to leave the Depot and in the winter, starting the buses up on a cold morning, left a thick cloud of unburnt diesel fumes inside the Depot. Normally, none of the buses started first time, adding to the cloud of fumes and making your eyes water and when breathed in, did you more harm than smoking 50 cigarettes a day.

The Inspector said, "You're with Smiler and your conductor is Dave 'Picker' Melane". I knew that Smiler was a driver renowned for his joking, but Picker?

I asked the Inspector, "Is Dave a guitar player?" Bill looked at me. I continued, "Well, with a name like Picker!".

"Oh gawd", said Bill (gawd was his favourite expression for any surprises or if things went wrong). He burst out laughing, then coughing, still without removing his pipe. "E's called Picker because e stands at the front of the bus and picks his nose". So, that was what Inspector Buxton meant when he told us to keep our noses clean. I left Bill coughing and spluttering and made my way to Bus 252, to begin 11 happy years with Bournemouth Transport.

We ran empty to pick up our route, No. 23 - Tuckton Bridge, Fisherman's Walk, Boscombe, Lansdowne to Bournemouth Square. On Leyland Atlanteans, the front doors were operated by the driver and on the way to start our service, the driver – Smiler – said, "I'll operate the doors". He continued, "Do you know why this bus is called the 'Fizzer'?".

17

"No", I said.

"The number 252 was an Army charge sheet. If you committed an offence in the forces, you were put on a 252 Charge or in Army slang - Fizzer", was the reply.

Dave the conductor said, "Move round the bus as fast as you can, we'll have a three bell load on this one".

"What's a three bell load?"

"Don't you know? Didn't they explain the bell codes in Training School. The trouble is they keep cutting the days down. When I started, you had a week in school, before you went on the road".

Smiler said, "What were the old horse buses like?".

Dave said, "Right. The conductor's bell code. Pushing the red button once, means stop. Twice means go. Three times means, full right up and that means you do not stop to pick up passengers, until somebody wants to get off. Four times - emergency (if you are getting attacked). Five times - I need a pint!".

Dave then explained the stages on my Fare Chart ie Tuckton Bridge, Cranleigh Road School and so on, then Fisherman's Walk, ending at the Square. Each fare stage was numbered and all the conductor had to do was set the appropriate number on the 'Setright' ticket machine and the amount and ring the ticket off. Dave said, "Any ones you can't find, give me a shout. The regular passengers know the fare, but if you start shouting, they will know you don't know the fares, deliberately give you the wrong money and over-ride – that why the Inspectors check tickets".

I started on the top deck and in those days smoking was allowed. The air could become thick with cigarette smoke and being a non-smoker, my eyes used to quickly smart and throat sting. The 23 Route is a short, busy trip and I stayed upstairs collecting fares, the whole way to Bournemouth Square. Dave stood on the platform collecting all the downstairs fares. He never moved and I wondered the wisdom of the Bus Company starting a new conductor in the rush hour, instead of in the middle of the morning when it was quieter?

Due to the morning rush hour, we were late reaching Bournemouth Square and turned straight round and went out on 22 Route (Bournemouth Square to Hengistbury Head), which was fairly busy. By this time the heavy 'Setright' weighed a ton and the heavy leather cash bag which, full of coins, dragged my shoulder down and the strap was cutting into my shoulder. Later, I would learn how to get rid of loose change to passengers and cash up on the move.

By this time, I had started running up and down the stairs and I was covered in perspiration. At this point, an Inspector boarded the bus and spoke to Dave, who had not moved from the front of the bus the whole time. "How's he doing, Dave?"

"Alright, but he will have to move a bit quicker if he's going to make a good conductor – like me!"

So ended day one!

"It's my student conductor!", the voice of Colin greeted me as I boarded Bus 254 on the second day of my hands-on training. "How did you get on with Picker yesterday?"

"Alright, but does he ever move from the front of the bus?"

"Only when it's time to get off", laughed Colin. "Today, I'll show you how the job *should* be done and give you a few tips."

We were on early duty 'main roads', so-called because route numbers 20, 21, 22 and 23 covered the main routes to Somerford, Christchurch, Tuckton Bridge, and Hengistbury Head. 'Side Roads' was a term used for routes 3, 5 and 6, which covered places such as Kinson, Bear Cross and Cunningham Crescent. During the early morning rush hour, trips from Bournemouth Square outward were not too busy, but coming back into the Square was always busy with people on their way to work. On the outward journeys, Colin left me to go round the bus on my own and get used to the fare stages. On inward journeys, Colin stayed on the top deck of the bus, as that was where all the fare dodgers and over-riding passengers went. It was easy to handle the lower deck, because there were less seats. The driver operated the doors, using the door control on the gear change box in his cab.

Half-past nine came and we had a 45 minute break in the canteen. "This is where your education begins", said Colin. I watched as the conductor in front of us in the queue in the canteen, ordered eggs, bacon, mushrooms, tomatoes, fried bread, beans, chips, bread and butter and tea! "He's having a 'Cunningham' breakfast", said Colin.

"What's that?"

When we sat down, Colin explained. "Some conductors fiddle the fares. They either don't issue tickets, or give the passenger a penny ticket for a 20 pence fare. One conductor's named 'Tortoise', because he's so slow collecting the fares!". Colin went on, "When his bus is full up leaving the Square, he waits until the Lansdowne before collecting fares and, of course, by this time, people are already starting to get off. He also rings his tickets off slowly if there are a lot of people and they either give him the money and dash off, or leave it on the tray next to the driver. He will ring off a couple of penny tickets to make it look good and push the rest of the money into his bag. He works downstairs for as long as he can and by this time, people are coming downstairs, putting their fares on the driver's tray and getting off. He then comes along and puts the money in his bag. He's being doing this for years and that's why he has never put in for driving – he makes more money than a driver, without the responsibility".

Colin continued, "Now Ian Cunningham is the General Manager, so it's his money, because he is in charge of the Bus Company. So, we call a conductor ordering a full breakfast a 'Cunningham', because on our wages you could not afford it every day".

"How is it that the Inspectors haven't caught him?", I asked.

"They know he does it, but it's proving it. He's crafty. Never leaves a penny ticket on the floor – always puts them in his pocket. The Inspectors once took a bus out of service and checked every used ticket on the floor and in the used ticket box and never found *one* penny ticket. A penny ticket should never be issued as there not any penny fares in the fare chart!".

This conductor in later years, went on to become a one-man–operated bus driver – an OMO – and was caught by an Inspector with two dud tickets and dismissed. He went on to win his appeal and was re-instated. Personally, I found most crews were honest and only a few resorted to fiddling the Company.

Colin then went on to explain that Inspectors were called 'Jumpers', although this was nothing to do with kangaroos or athletics! Inspectors knew all the tricks, having started as conductors, then changing to driving, although as one Inspector remarked later, I was able to show, even them, some new tricks!

Some 'Jumpers' used to hide in shop doorways and even behind trees! We had to watch out particularly for Dave 'The Fox', whose speciality was only appearing at night, working a late shift. Seeing all and saying nothing, you didn't know he was watching you, until he boarded your bus and had a quiet word in your ear.

The crews had an early warning system when a 'Jumper' was about, the driver of the bus

Yellow Bus Time Table

BOURNEMOUTH TRANSPORT

30th NOVEMBER 1980
UNTIL FURTHER NOTICE

10p

STAFF COPY

coming in the opposite direction, jerking his thumb backwards, similar to a hitchhiker. The driver had to ensure that he was not running early (ahead of the timetable), the routes having timing points and it was a bookable offence to run early, although *not* late. As one 'Jumper' remarked that "there are 100 excuses for running late, but not one for running early". Meanwhile, the conductor would nip round the bus to make sure he had collected all the fares and that nobody was over-riding, although this was impossible with a bus full of passengers.

It was the conductor's responsibility to ensure that there were no over-riders and it was the conductor who got into trouble – not the passenger. The passenger would simply say that they had told the conductor when paying the fare, that they wanted to get off at Fisherman's Walk, instead of the truth, that they had asked for an 18 pence fare from the Square, which took them to Pokesdown station! The Inspector would book the conductor for this offence ie details of the incident would be written down by the 'Jumper' and submitted to the Traffic Office in his Daily Report. The conductor would get a note from the Traffic Office two days later, asking for an explanation and he would reply, saying that the passenger had only asked for an 18 pence ticket. The Traffic Office would write back, telling him that in future he must ask the passenger's destination and to be more careful in future. If the conductor had been reported in the past for the same offence, he could be stopped one or two weeks merit bonus. As I said at the start of this narration, the job did not run on tea – it ran on bits of paper!

---

25 / 68

ROSCOMBE—WESTBOURNE
Via Ashley Road, Holdenhurst Road, Lansdowne, Old Christchurch Road, Hinton Road, Westover Road, Gervis Place, The Square, Commercial Road, Poole Hill, Poole Road and Seamoor Road.

25 / 68

BOSCOMBE—PARKSTONE—ALDERNEY
Via Ashley Road, Holdenhurst Road, Lansdowne, Bath Road, Westover Road, as Service 25 to Seamoor Road, then via Poole Road, Ashley Road, Upper Parkstone, Sea View Road, Grove Road, Cranbrook Road, Cynthia Road, Brixey Road, Rossmore Road, Stanfield Church, Herbert Avenue and Ringwood Road to Francis Avenue.

MONDAYS TO SATURDAYS

	B am	am	B am	am	am	am	B am	am	am	B am	am	B am	am
HAVILAND ROAD WEST													
Capstone Place	6 28	6 58	7 28	7 43	7 58	8 13	8 25	8 37	8 49	9 01	9 13	9 25	
Bournemouth Rail Station	6 35	7 05	7 35	7 50	8 05	8 20	8 32	8 44	8 56	9 08	9 20	9 32	
SQUARE (Woolworths)	6 39	7 09	7 39	7 54	8 09	8 24	8 36	8 48	9 00	9 12	9 24	9 36	
Westbourne (Seamoor Rd.)	6 51	7 20	7 51	8 06	8 21	8 36	8 48	9 00	9 12	9 24	9 36	9 48	
Sea View	6 58	7 27	7 58	8 13	8 28	8 43	8 55	9 07	9 19	9 31	9 43	9 55	
Cranbrook Rd./Cynthia Rd.	7 09		8 09					9 12					
Good Shepherd Church	7 13		8 13					9 18					
ALDERNEY (Waterworks)	7 19		8 19					9 22					
	7 25		8 26					9 28					
								9 34					

		Then at these mins. past each hour						pm	pm		Then at these mins. past each hour			pm	B pm
HAVILAND ROAD WEST															
Capstone Place	37	49	01	13	25			5 49	6 02		34	02		1002	1034
Bournemouth Rail Station	44	56	08	20	32			5 56	6 09		41	09		1009	1041
SQUARE (Woolworths)	00	12	24	36				6 00	6 13		45	13		1013	1045
Westbourne (Seamoor Rd.)	07	19	31	43	55			6 12	6 23		57	23		1023	1057
Sea View	18							6 19	6 30		04	30		1030	1104
Cranbrook Rd./Cynthia Rd.	22										15				1115
Good Shepherd Church	28										19				1119
ALDERNEY (Waterworks)	34										25				1125
											30				1130

	am	am	am	am	am	am	am	am				pm	pm
ALDERNEY (Waterworks)			7 15					8 15				27	
Good Shepherd Church			7 23					8 23				35	
Cranbrook Rd./Cynthia Rd.			7 29					8 29	Then at these mins. past each hour			41	
Sea View			7 33					8 33				45	
Westbourne (Poole Rd.)	7 05	7 30	7 47	8 05	8 20	8 35	8 47	8 59				59	
SQUARE (Avenue Rd.)	7 15	7 40	7 57	8 15	8 30	8 45	8 57	9 09				11	
Bournemouth Rail Station	7 22	7 47	8 04	8 22	8 37	8 52	9 04	9 16				23 35 47 59	
Capstone Place	7 26	7 51	8 08	8 26	8 41	8 56	9 08	9 20	each			28 40 52 04 16	
HAVILAND ROAD WEST	7 33	7 58	8 15	8 33	8 48	9 03	9 15	9 27	hour			39 51 03 15 27	

	pm	pm	pm	pm							pm	pm
ALDERNEY (Waterworks)	5 27			6 27							1030	
Good Shepherd Church	5 35			6 35				30			1035	
Cranbrook Rd./Cynthia Rd.	5 41			6 41				35			1041	
Sea View	5 45			6 45	Then at these mins. past each hour			41			1045	
Westbourne (Poole Rd.)	5 59	6 11	6 31	6 56				45			1056	
SQUARE (Avenue Rd.)	6 09	6 21	6 39	7 06		31	56		until		1031	1106
Bournemouth Rail Station	6 16	6 28	6 46	7 13		39	06				1039	1113
Capstone Place	6 20	6 32	6 50	7 17		46	13				1046	1117
HAVILAND ROAD WEST	6 27	6 39	6 57	7 24		50	17				1050	1117
						57	24				1057	1124

CODE   B – Via Bath Road, NOT Old Christchurch Road

(continued on next page)

22

Many a passenger has been perplexed when the conductor, having been tipped off by a bus coming in the other direction, that a 'Jumper' was waiting up the road, turns to the passengers and says, "Have your tickets ready for inspection - an Inspectors round the corner". Some passengers used to think I was a clairvoyant!

While Colin and I were sat in the canteen talking, a driver sat at the next table said, "Colin. You know you fixed me up with a date with Hungry Hilda. You said she was insatiable. Well, I took her out on my day off yesterday and she was insatiable. *She never stopped bloody eating!* Cost me a fortune. When you fixed me up, I thought she was insatiable for *sex*!".

Turning to me and laughing, Colin said "Hungry Hilda is one of our Bus Bikes. Pop groups have Groupies – bus crews have Bus Bikes – they give you a quick peddle! Watch out for Midnight Mary! Good looking bloke like you, will soon be parted from his trousers" (Midnight Mary was so nick-named because she offered her favours to crews working late shifts).

Colin then went on to tell me the story of a one-man-operated bus driver, who had spent his lay-over time at Hengistbury Head – laying over Midnight Mary on the back seat upstairs with the lights out! A passenger waiting to board the bus, on finding the doors closed and the bus in darkness, became rather irritable. He started banging on the doors and the driver having had his amorous lay-over interrupted, strode downstairs, started the engine and drove off, leaving the passenger behind. The resulting complaint and memo from the Traffic Office was answered by the driver, who said that he had not seen the passenger at the bus stop, neither had he heard him banging on the doors, because at the time he had cotton wool in his ears, due to an ear complaint.

I was also tipped off by Colin about Somerford Lil, who lived in Somerford and the fact that her ex-husband was a bus driver. I was warned that if other busmen saw you talking to any Bus Bikes, they assumed you were chatting them up!

The day passed quickly enough and I was shown how to cash-up on the move, thus reducing the weight of the heavy bag which cut into your shoulder.

'HAVE YOUR FARES READY, PLEEZ!'

My first duty conducting a bus on my own, was arriving to sign-on for a late turn duty at Mallard Road Depot. Most late turns started in the Square and after drawing a heavy metal box containing my 'setright' machine, I retired to the so-called 'Rest Room', which at that time of day was usually empty. In the mornings, the room was a babble of conversation, with mostly staff complaining about the job and the passengers.

First, I checked my machine, to make sure it had a full roll of tickets and also a spare roll as standby. Next, I counted my float, five-pound floats being issued by the Company and paid back at the end of your service with the Company.

Now it was time to look at the Rule book and turning to the section on collecting fares, I read: *'FARE COLLECTION: When you are in service carry out your fares collection and other duties in the manner you have been taught in the Training School. Don't try to invent ways of your own. Try to collect every fare and stop every overrider'*. This was an impossible job and during my service, I only came across one conductor who could achieve this. *'If you make a mistake in the fare and the passenger challenges it, don't bluff it out, acknowledge it in a proper manner and put things right.'* Later, I was to find out how many arguments could take place over a penny!

'If a passenger cannot pay his fare, ask for some form of identity and complete a 'non-payment' form.' This paragraph was to cause all sorts or problems. It was designed to help a passenger who had lost a purse, or a child who had no money to get home. Human nature being what it is, as soon as the word got around with some sections of the community, it was seen as free travel on the buses. After being issued with a 'non-payment' form, the passenger was supposed to either call or send the money owed to Mallard Road. Few did and often Inspectors' time was spent trying to find a house with the name of a passenger and find there was no such street.

One Inspector told me, he had called at a certain address to collect a string of unpaid fare slips and was invited by the lady who opened the door to him, to go upstairs and work them off. However, having a weak heart and being a heavy breather, he declined. The lady was very upset at being rejected and her parting shot was, "Well, the last Inspector agreed a ride for a ride!".

It reached the stage where some people were making a living out of giving false names and addresses and the Company eventually issued a list of names of people who had not paid in the past. *I never knew there were so many Smiths living in Bournemouth!*

To give an example, a fella got on my bus and said, "Take my address. I've got no money and I've got to get home".

After writing it down, I said to my driver, "Stop the bus!". Turning to the passenger, I said, "Welcome home – that's your road there!".

"What?", he said, "I'm going to the Square".

"Not on this bus. The non-payment is designed to get you home. It's not valid on outward journeys!"

Yobbos on the last bus, soon cottoned onto the idea of free travel. On late buses, you would go upstairs (yobbos always travelled upstairs) and a group of them would say, "Got no money, mate. Take my name and address".

Being younger, stronger and more foolish in those days, I would shout, "Driver. Stop the bus. Four getting off". I would then say, "Have you four lads enjoyed a good drink in the town?".

"Yes mate."

"And you didn't save enough money for your bus fare?"

With the bus stopped and the rest of the passengers shouting, "Pay up! We want to get home", the yobbos would either cough-up, or other yobbos on the bus would chip-in to pay the fare. As they got off the bus, they would say, "We'll remember *you*".

I would reply, "Don't remember me. Remember to save enough money for your fare home".

One day, an elderly tramp got on my bus. "Take my name and address", he said.

"What address?", I said, "Would it be Mr. Smith - no fixed abode?".

"No", he said and gave a posh name and address in Canford Cliffs, upon which I invited him to get off and use his Rolls (cheese or ham!).

He blustered in front of the other passengers, "I'm getting off this bus, going into the phone box and reporting you – I've got your number".

"Just one thing", I said, "If you have no money, how are you going to phone the Company? They will not accept reverse phone charges, as well as free rides".

Once when I asked a passenger, "Can you identify yourself?", he pulled out a mirror, looked in it and said, "That's me!".

One old lady got on the bus in tears one day and said, "I've lost my purse!".

"I'm sorry to hear that. Was he ill for long?", I asked. I told her not to worry and paid her fare. There is a happy ending to this story. Her purse was handed in and she paid me back and until she died, I received a Christmas card every year, sent to Mallard Road Depot.

Returning to the Rule Book, another section read: *'Check all coins received. The Department will not accept any foreign or counterfeit coins you collect'*. To this day, I do not know why bus conductors are seen as a Foreign Exchange? So many people try and work off dimes, marks, dustbin lids, or any form of currency on the poor old conductor. The usual trick is to conceal the foreign coins in a handful of loose change and on a busy bus, most conductors will put the coins straight into their bags. Only later will they find that they have a handful of coins the Company will not accept. So, you have to pay your own money to cover them and next duty, work them back onto the passengers with a handful of change. Some coins have been doing the rounds for years!

These transactions normally take place on full buses and one day, two fellas were sitting together, laughing. When I went to collect their fares, one gave me an Irish 50p piece. "Can't accept that", I said, "It's not legal tender in this country. You'll have to catch an Irish bus. We only have two in our fleet and this is not one of them". (Bournemouth's first-rear-engined buses were two Daimler 'Fleetlines', built in Belfast for use in Corporation service in Belfast. They arrived at Mallard Road Depot in full Belfast Corporation maroon livery, but were quickly repainted in Yellow Bus colours.)

The person sitting next to the passenger giving me the Irish 50p piece said, "I work in a bank and can assure you it is legal tender". As he was dressed in overalls, covered in dried paint, I was not convinced! However, as my Rule Book stated *'avoid arguments and try to avoid provocation'*, I gave him a ticket for 20p and his change.

The fella in the overalls – still smirking – gave me a pound and said, "20 pence please". I gave him his ticket and change, including the 50p piece. He said, "What's this? I'm not accepting Irish money!".

I said, "*You* were the one who said it was legal tender" and walked away.

Back to the first day on my own, in the Rest Room, I was sitting engrossed in my Rule Book, when I heard a voice say, "Are you Tommy Steele?".

Since I was the only person sitting in the room, I said, "Hope so. In fact, I'm the *real* Tommy Steele".

"Well, I'm your mate – Reg Harding. Is this your first trip?", he asked.

"Yes and I'm nervous."

"You'll be alright, if you get them in early". He explained, "Start collecting the fares before the bus departs. That way, you will be on top".

"What! Upstairs?"

Reg ignored my joke and said, "I've had some duff mates lately".

"Thanks", I said.

Reg continued, "This job will be all one-man-operated soon".

Some routes were already OMO-operated and some drivers worked both OMO buses and crew-operated turns. A lot of drivers, after training, swapped their duties with another OMO driver who had a crew turn, because they did not like OMO operation, despite the pay being higher. The Corporation wanted one-man buses throughout the service, but it took six years - 12th April 1986 - before the last conductor hung up his bag. The Company, to entice the Union to go OMO-operation, offered a bonus, payable every six months, to all staff and slowly, route by route, all fell to OMO operation. The Union was against the practice, but there was little they could do. What happened to the old conductors who could not – or would not – go in for driving? They were pensioned off and a way of life went for ever and stress crept into the job.

On 12th April 1986, the fun went out of the job. No more jokes, such as, "Do you stop at the Royal Bath, conductor?".

"What! On my wages!"

Passenger tendering fare: "Peter's Hill".

"Sorry to hear that, luv. What's wrong with him?".

Conductor to passengers: "Don't ring the bell. The drivers an ex-boxer and every time he hears it, he comes out fighting".

No more calling out the fare stages: "Fisherman's Walk" or "Fisherman's Run"; "Derby Road, red light district of Bournemouth".

Or, helping old ladies on and off a bus; lifting shopping trollies, so heavy, they seem filled with bricks; helping mums with pushchairs; sorting out a bus queue, which is an art - today, waiting for a bus soon becomes a free-for-all when it arrives. A good crew, working together, could operate a bus smart and also have a good laugh. Going to work was a pleasure, as I will relate later on

Recalling my mates on the buses, Reg proved a good, steady mate, helping me by keeping control of the doors and starting-up as soon as the passengers had boarded, without waiting for me to ring the bell. He was a stickler for doing his job correctly, to such an extent, he ran to time even on the last trip of the day.

A busmen's saying was, that the last trip of the night 'is your own'. Mind you, the Inspectors did not see it that way! Buses would leave on time from the Square, stay on time to Boscombe Arcade, which was the last major picking-up point, then go like a bat out of hell, running early, sometimes up to four minutes by Tuckton Bridge (if you had a fast bus and few stops). Very few people caught the bus after Fisherman's Walk, so if you were an intending passenger and came out on time to catch the bus at, say Tuckton Bridge to Christchurch, you missed it. This frequently resulted in complaints to the Company.

From time-to-time, the Inspectors would have a crackdown and wait at timing points and if the bus arrived early, the driver (not the conductor) was booked. Seems strange, when you come to think of it, because the conductor is in charge of the bus, not the driver? Some of the ploys used by Inspectors to catch drivers were funny – better than 'Blakey' in the 'On The Buses' TV sitcom!

An Inspector would, perhaps, be seen in another part of Bournemouth and the grapevine amongst the drivers would soon pass the word round where he was operating. So, if he was seen in Kinson, it was impossible for him to get over to Tuckton Bridge in time to catch the last bus running early, using the timetable buses. But, some Inspectors would have their car handy and slip across to Tuckton Bridge or other points. This was considered unsporting, but to be fair, was only used on drivers that consistently ran early.

The Inspectors would ask to see the the driver's watch to check the time, but crafty drivers would either set their watches early, so it agreed with the timetable, or have two watches, one with the correct time and the other set early for the Inspector. When asked, why he had not set his watch with the Inspectors' clock in the Square, he would state either that he had, or that he had forgot.

One of my drivers had a watch with a Mickey Mouse face, minus one of Mickey's hands. That trick 'the hands fallen off' worked once with each Inspector, until the driver showed it twice to the same Inspector, who booked him for taking the Mickey out of him!

One Inspector, waiting in the dark at Hengistbury Head, for the last Number 22 to arrive, had to walk home when the driver running with an empty bus, did not go down the Broadway, but carried straight on into the Depot. When he got a memo from the office asking why he did not complete the route, he stated that his bus was empty and nobody could get on because it was the end of the route. In his reply, he said he was only thinking of the Company and saving them money on fuel. The Office wrote back and commended him saving the Company money and also helped him to save more money by stopping him four weeks merit bonus. After that episode, Inspectors no longer waited for the last Number 22. "After all", as one of the Inspector said to me, "There is a limit to our loyalty to the Company and walking home is not one of them!".

Remember at the beginning, I mentioned that there were excuses for running late, but none for running early? One driver was caught running five minutes early. He knew he was going to lose a lot of money from his merit bonus, so he decided to consult another driver named John, known as 'The Barrack Room Lawyer'. John could compose beautiful letters of reply to his and other's wrongdoings, although usually, this was not enough to touch the heart of the Traffic Superintendent, who over the years had seen nearly every type of excuse (I was only able to put one past him once in 10 years).

John composed a letter and told the driver to write using his own handwriting (the Office knew John's by heart!) that the reason he was running early during his last trip, was because he was dashing to find a toilet. The driver who was in trouble, liked this suggestion and said that it was also partly true and he wrote in his letter that the diarrhea had started when he saw the Inspector. Anyway, such an excuse could not fail and he gladly paid John's fee for composing the letter of excuse, the going rate being buying John a huge meal in the canteen.

The only flaw in the story was that the Traffic Superintendent - David Chalk lived in Bournemouth and knew the route well. In his reply confirming a substantial stoppage of bonus, Superintendent Chalk pointed out that the driver had already passed public toilets, a short distance before he was caught out. Memos were read out in the canteen to other crews and one wag remarked, "That's another way of putting *caught short*!".

Reg Harding, in all the time I worked with him, never ran early, even waiting for the correct time at the terminus on the last bus, before proceeding 'running empty' to Depot. For that reason, he was not a popular mate!

TOMMY'S TICKLER!

A driver was driving a single-decker bus between several seaside towns, when early one morning, a passenger got on and stayed all day sat on the back seat, eating crisps, cakes and drinking soft drinks. He also had a little sing-song in between. When he eventually got off at the end of the day, the driver asked him if he had enjoyed the trip? "Oh yes", the man said, "This is my firm's annual seaside outing".
When the driver pointed out that there was only one of him, the man replied, "I know – I'm self-employed!".

SING-AS-WE-GO!

Once your feet got used to conducting, it was a very enjoyable job. Nowadays, you need to travel to London to see a good conductor at work, but there are not many of the old school of conductors left. They were always making jokes, such as, reaching the end of the journey and shouting "Aldgate East – All get out!". Questions, such as, "Does this bus go over Tower Bridge?". "Hope so madam, otherwise we will all get our feet wet".

Singing bus conductors and drivers (remember Matt Monroe?) were common in those days. I decided to make my passengers happier by singing. Mind you, I enjoyed the job and would walk up and down the bus, singing. I may have cheered the passengers up, but not my Welsh driver, who said, "Hey boyo. If you keep singing, you be working this bus by yourself".

"Is it true you Welshmen sing all through the night?", I enquired.

"We do boyo."

"Do you get a sore throat afterwards?" My singing always caused a reaction among the passengers and once singing 'Have you ever been kissed in the moonlight?', I turned to a haughty young lady and joked, "Have you ever been kissed in the moonlight?".

"Mind your own business", she replied, then added, "Are you in the habit of speaking to ladies you don't know?".

"Yes", I said, "Because the ones I know, won't speak to me!".

My song, 'When you're smiling, the whole bus smiles with you', went down better with the evening passengers, than with the early morning ones on their way to work. It could also be fatal among your mates in the canteen, comments such as, "You wouldn't sing if you had the miserable so and so's I've had this morning" frequently coming in my direction.

I found during all my years of bus work – and talking to busmen today – that the passengers are the enemy. I once worked with a driver, who said, "This job would be alright if we never had to carry passengers!". Once when I conducted with him and we had a full bus, he showed me his party trick. Turning to me, he said, "I bet I can get all the passengers sitting downstairs to agree with me, watch this". He said loudly to me, *"You passengers are a lot of silly blighters!"* and with that, he put his foot on the brake hard, then quickly off several times, so that all the passengers heads nodded in agreement! He used to do this several times and if you laughed, he would give you an encore.

My mates did not take kindly to my singing in the canteen and one day, they made out signs similar to the 'No smoking' signs, saying 'No singing zone'.

'She's got a ticket to ride', I sang and asked, "Have you all got tickets to ride?", which made a change from "Fares Please".

Tickets play a big part in bus work and some of the tricks passengers played to avoid paying their fare were unique, although after you have been in the job for a time, you learn to spot them. One-man-operated buses have prevented fare evasion, but increased overriding. When there were conductors on the buses, they would spot overriders and a good conductor would have a good memory. One conductor – Herbie Wilson – had such a good memory, he could spot people going past their fare stage even with a full bus (more about Herbie later).

Let me reveal some of the tricks the passengers used to pull. Passengers would throw their tickets on the floor of the bus when getting off at their destination and yobbos who were boarding would pick them up, then put them in their mouth and chew them up. When challenged to show their ticket, they would take a soggy ticket out of their mouth. Obviously all the information printed on the ticket would be unreadable and I would say, "You'll have to pay again, because if an Inspector gets on and asks to see your ticket, he won't *swallow* that" (many an Inspector has been offered a soggy ticket to check!). This is where a good memory comes in useful, as a conductor will remember if the passengers had paid their fares.

Yobbos are easy to spot, as they stand out when they get on the bus and usually go straight upstairs and sit in the back seats (and write on them in those days when seats were made of plastic). They do not realise it's easy to remember and after asking them for their fare, they produce a soggy ticket. I would say, "Try eating *Readers Digest* after you have paid for your ticket". If they refused to pay, you rang the bell and shouted "Three to get off, driver!". I've had many a fist waved at me as we pulled away from the stop and a stream of four-letter words after putting them off. Some would kick the side of the bus, which never bothered me, as it was easier to get the bus repaired than their foot!

If you didn't have a good memory – I always remembered the adage 'If in doubt, leave it out' – for it was not only yobbos that used the ticket-in-mouth-trick. People from all walks of life would resort to fare dodging. I very often used to think, how do they make the buses pay? The Corporation was not only being cheated by *some* conductors, but also *some* passengers, although in all my time working on the buses, I cannot remember a single passenger being prosecuted for fare evasion.

Another trick - and judging by the numbers I caught, used by ladies and elderly gentlemen – was to be reading a book with half a ticket (either from a previous journey or a ticket picked up from the floor) showing. Conductors, seeing the ticket sticking out of the book and the passenger reading and not making eye contact, would walk on. It was impossible on a busy bus, with people getting on and off, to collect all the fares, let alone keep tabs on the passengers. Some Inspectors, after checking passenger's tickets and finding one or two uncollected fares, would sympathise with you, because they knew some passengers deliberately evaded paying their fare.

One Inspector, called Brian, a silver-haired, Cary Grant (the film star) look-alike, checked my bus. He came downstairs, smacked the back of my head with a fare chart and said, "Two uncollected fares and one overrider!". He could have reported me, but preferred to dispense instant justice instead.

It was Brian who solved a mystery, by telling me why in the Summer, while working the Number 35 route, on leaving Cemetery Junction, en route down Wimborne Road to the Square, bus staff, who had been travelling downstairs, went upstairs for the short journey to the Square via Richmond Hill. It transpires that along Wimborne Road, was a garden with a high fence. In the garden, was a well-endowed young lady, who used to sunbathe topless. When she heard a bus coming, she would get up and stretch herself. Apparently, with the amount of people on the top deck, the bus used to tilt! One driver even got one of his mates to take over driving between Cemetery Junction and the top of Richmond Hill, so he could go upstairs!

Before leaving the subject of fare evasion, I must tell you another trick used by two or more passengers. You could be upstairs or downstairs, it didn't really matter. You went to collect a fare – "Fares, please" - and the immortal words would be heard from the passenger: "'E's got it!".

"Got what?"- I used to think it was some form of illness!

"Me fare."

"Where's 'E?"

"Upstairs" or "downstairs", the passenger would reply, depending on where you asked for the fare.

By the time you went upstairs to find ''E', the passenger had got off without paying *or* you would find ''E' after a detailed description, who said, "No. I'm not paying *his* fare. I thought he was paying *mine*!".

The first time this happened to me, I was up and down the stairs like a yo-yo, in the process missing several fares from people who got off without paying and after conducting for several weeks and falling for the ''E' trick, I learnt to say,

"Go up and get it from 'E"

Due to the Corporation's policy of not prosecuting fare dodgers (I found out the Corporation thought it might give them a bad name, would you believe!), I decided to hand out my own form of justice and to make passengers think twice about using me to pull a fast one. You got to know regular fare dodgers and I waited until this one got off before confronting him on the pavement and, having a loud voice, showed him up in front of a queue of people. He never got on my bus again and several times I spotted him at bus stops looking to see who the conductor was.

One of the most satisfying fare dodgers I caught, was a young man sitting upstairs at the front of the bus. It was full and I had collected my fares downstairs, then started on the top deck. "Fares, please".

The young man said, "I've paid!".

"Show me your ticket."

"I've lost it."

You certainly have mate, I thought. "How much did you pay and where are you going?"

"Can't remember, but it was a return."

That's it! I had him. *We did not do returns.* He went to get off, but I stood in front of him and in a very loud voice said, "You're a liar! We don't issue returns. Unless you've been sitting in two places at once, I've collected all the fares downstairs and you're the first fare I've collected upstairs. Now let me have your fare".

"Got no money", he replied.

"If you had told me that when I asked for your fare, I would have issued you with an uncollected fare slip and you could have paid later."

The woman sitting next to him said, "I would have paid your fare, but not now you've tried to get the conductor into trouble, should an Inspector have got on".

With the whole top deck looking at him, he walked past me, head bowed and got off.

TWO FINGERS

Signing on for early duty one day, the Mallard Road Depot duty Inspector – 'Bill the Pipe' – handed me a brown envelope. Through the pipe, clenched firmly in his mouth (rumour had it that he never removed it, even to eat), he mumbled, "Been a naughty boy again, 'ave we?".

"No Bill – it's my promotion to Inspector."

Bill choked and in between gasping and coughing, spluttered, "You'll never make an Inspector, as long as I've got an 'ole in my arse!".

"Thanks for the compliment, Bill."

My repartee with Bill was legendary and although he always appeared gruff, he always had a twinkle in his eye. He was right about me becoming an Inspector, though. I did put in for a vacancy once and the laughter from the Office could be heard all over Mallard Road Depot as they typed the standard reply: *'Your application is receiving attention'*, my application being neatly filed in the waste paper basket!

Having been a joker all my life, trying to act serious as an Inspector would have been difficult. The job of Inspector was not an easy one, because you were halfway between your former mates – the bus crews – and the management.

One Inspector once said to me, "We are the eyes of the management - we let them see what's going on".

My reply was, "Pity they don't come out on a bus and and, perhaps, they would open their eyes".

I don't wish to give the wrong impression, there were some good Inspectors, of course and some naïve ones. One once said to me, "If all busmen were like you, the Company wouldn't need Inspectors".

Brown envelopes were the standard communication between the Traffic Office and the staff and judging by the amount of open, discarded envelopes in the waste bins or on the floor of the so-called 'Rest Room' at the Depot, the envelope suppliers must have made a fortune. It's a funny thing over the years, that during my visits to many bus crews' rest rooms, there's always been more rubbish on the floor than in the bins. I always wonder their homes must be like?

Busmen would crowd someone, who had just collected his envelope and say, "Open it up. Let's see what you have been up to?" The purpose of enclosing a Traffic Office memo in an envelope was to keep it confidential, but some busmen took great delight in reading out their crimes, against what they saw as authority. I should explain that a copy of all memos and the action taken was placed on the busman's file at the Mallard Road office. It was referred to as 'Your Record' and over the years, my record became so heavy, that it took two people to lift it out of the filing cabinet.

I used to tell people that I had a criminal record. If you appeared before the Traffic Superintendent, he would have the advantage of looking up your misdeeds over the years, as the records were better than the busman's memory.

One brown envelope opened in the Rest Room by a driver called Bill, caused quite a crowd to gather round. As different busmen came in during their rest periods, Bill had to read the memo out aloud several times, roars of laughter and admiration greeting each reading. The contents of the memo dealt with the fact that Bill had been operating a one-man bus and, as often happens, he could not get the bus into the kerb to let a long queue of people board. Cars had been parked on the bus stop, which left him no option, but to stop the bus with the back of the vehicle stuck out into the middle of the road, almost touching a traffic bollard.

So, the road was blocked and being a one-man-operated service, this meant that Bill was taking the fares as the passengers boarded, which took some time. While he was doing this, an irate motorist started blowing his horn and after several blasts, Bill opened the cab window and stuck two fingers out giving him a 'V' sign. The fella jumped out of his car just as Bill drove off and looking in his mirror, he saw him write down the number of the bus.

Drivers can always be traced by the time, route and bus number and this time the Traffic Office didn't waste any time, for the person making the complaint was a Bournemouth councillor!

"Treated like gods", grumbled one of the assembled drivers.

"Did you know that they stood to attention in the Traffic Office, when this complaint came in over the telephone?" said another.

Of course, Bournemouth Transport was run by Bournemouth Council and as Bill disclosed his 'crime' to his mates, he was given all sorts of advice:

"You'll get life for this, Bill."

"You'll lose more than two weeks' merit bonus for *two* fingers!"

"Go sick for, say, two years? It might have blown over by then."

"No way you'll get off this one."

At that moment, John (the busmens' barrack room lawyer) walked in and Bill showed him the memo, saying, "Even you can't get me out of this one!".

There was silence in the room, while John studied the memo. He smiled, saying, "Bill. I have the answer". The crowd waited with bated breath.

"Come on then, John."

Earlier in the book, I explained that John's fee for writing convincing replies to the Traffic Office was a dinner purchased in the canteen and - savouring the moment – he said, "*Two* fingers will cost you *two dinners, plus sweets*!".

"Agreed", said Bill, "It's cheaper than several weeks merit money being stopped".

"Or hanging!", shouted on wag.

John said, "When you write your reply, you state that you thought of the safety of the passengers boarding, so you got the front of the bus into the kerb – write that in LARGE letters - the Office will like that!".

"But, we couldn't give a toss about the passengers", interrupted one busman.

"I know", said John, "But, what does the Rule Book say? *Always consider the safety and comfort of your passengers*. Now, the key point, you did *not* give the councillor the 'V' sign".

"But, I did!", said Bill.

"You did not. You indicated that you would only be two minutes boarding your passengers safely."

"Brilliant", said Bill, "If you were a woman, I'd marry you!".

"If I was a woman Bill, I wouldn't be composing letters. I'd be making more money doing something else ..."

"He's already in training", said one wag, "Screwing the Corporation".

"You should be at the Old Bailey", said a driver, with a look of admiration.

"In the dock!", said another.

Bill, needless to say, was out of the dock and on the slate in the canteen. John was in credit for two dinners, plus two sweets. "How did you get them?", asked the canteen assistant.

"Two fingers", replied John.

TOMMY'S TICKLERS!

A drunk gets on a bus and hands the conductor a £5.00 note.
"Where to, Sir?".
The drunk sways, looks round bleary-eyed and says, "Mars".
"That will be 90 pence, Sir. Change at Venus."
"I'm not that drunk, conductor, I want my change now."

Passenger complaining to conductor, after having an
argument with him.
"I don't like your attitude. I want your name, I'm going to
report you to the Bus Company."
"Wells Fargo, Sir."
"Is that your real name?" asked the passenger.
"No, Sir. That's my stage name!"

Passenger complaining after getting on the bus and finding
that the fares had gone up.
"Do you know, conductor. It's probably cheaper to fly
Concorde to the Lansdowne, than catch a bus?"
"Maybe, luv. But Concorde doesn't land at the Lansdowne!"

SMOKE GETS IN YOUR EYES

The only thing I did not like about working early turns, was cigarette smoke. Being a non-smoker, the first thing I did before the bus left the Depot, was to go upstairs and open all the sliding windows, to get some nice fresh air. I must point out, that in those days, smoking was permitted on the upper saloons (top deck), but not in the lower. In later years, a 'clippie' (woman conductor), told me a funny story about a fella, who got on a bus with a cigarette in his mouth unlit. The clippie walked up to him and said, "Hey! No smoking downstairs".

"I'm *not* smoking."

"You've got a cigarette in your mouth."

"I've got my shoes on, but I'm not walking."

"Do you want to get me into trouble?"

"Yes! What time do you finish?"

After the bus had left the Depot and ran empty to the first pick-up point, we would pick up the first passengers. Immediately, all the windows upstairs would be closed and the air filled with thick cigarette smoke. People would be coughing all over the place and even my uniform smelt of tobacco smoke!

One passenger who always got on first, used to go upstairs, shut all the windows, then light up and cough his ears off. I said to him one day, "Do cigarettes make you cough?".

"Only thing that does. I've tried cough sweets, but they don't work".

After a while, I discovered a trick that sometimes worked: open the windows only half-an-inch or so, so that the smokers didn't realise they were open. However, some seasoned smokers even spotted this ploy and closed them to ensure they had a better cough!

A few years ago, smoking was banned completely on buses and a good thing to, I say. If you had seen the mess on the floor of the upper saloon of a bus, on a wet day, after the bus had returned to the Depot, I am sure you would agree. I used to feel sorry for the bus cleaners, as sometimes it was so bad, that the top deck had to be hosed down!

Despite smoking being banned for the passengers, some bus crews thought it did not apply to them. It's an offence to smoke while driving a bus or coach and the Ministry of Transport take a very serious view of any driver caught smoking at the wheel.

Today, more one-man-operated drivers smoke, because of stress and because they are late reaching their return journey timing points, they smoke in the cab. During my OMO days, I've often taken a bus over and found the cab full of ash (turning on the demisters, can blow cigarette ash all over you!).

Two funny stories concerning crews smoking: A conductor having a quick drag while the bus was waiting in the Square, suddenly saw an Inspector bearing down on him. Panicking, he threw the cigarette - still alight - over his shoulder (some Inspectors would book any busman who smoked on the bus and this Inspector was one of them!). The cigarette landed on the back seat, which began smouldering. The Inspector getting on the bus, saw the smoke rising from the seat and said, "Do you know your back seats on fire?".

"You hum it and I'll try and sing it", said the conductor.

After extinguishing the smoke, turning to the conductor, the Inspector said, "I'm going to book you for smoking".

Having a quick mind, the conductor replied, "So, that's what he did with it! I've just put a passenger off for smoking". *He got away with it!*

A one-man driver, waiting at a terminus having his break, found two old ladies banging on his door to be let in (drivers do not like passengers being on the bus when they are trying to get some peace!). Being a cold, wet night, he let them on and sat in the cab finishing his cigarette. Two days later, he received a memo from the Traffic Office informing him the two ladies had reported him for smoking on the bus!

On one journey, we did not have many passengers to talk to and my driver was the 'Bogeyman'! He got this nickname because he always looked miserable and some of the more unkind busmen reckoned when he was off duty, he went around haunting houses! When there wasn't many passengers, the conductor sometimes used to spend his time talking to the driver at the front of the bus, standing under a printed notice which read: *'Do not speak to the driver or distract his attention'*. Talking to the 'Bogeyman' was like extracting teeth, as he always drove the bus staring straight ahead. I used to try joking with him: "Did you hear about the driver who got the sack for telling the passengers that the Inspectors are barmy?". I looked at the 'Bogeyman'. No reaction! I continued, "They sacked him for giving away company secrets". Still no reaction and I thought to myself. 'It's going to be a long shift tonight!'

We were working the last bus from the Square to Somerford. To make it worse, the 'Bogeyman' had spent the evening saying little and being a Monday night, we did not have a single passenger on board. It was like a morgue – just the right atmosphere for the 'Bogeyman' – and looking at him, I could imagine it!

Waiting at the bus stop at the Lansdowne was a passenger who had a hole as big as a cannon-ball in his jersey and as he got on, he was singing 'The last waltz'. "The Last Waltz on the last bus", I said.

"Do you fancy a dance?", said cannon-ball.

"Why not. It's been a miserable night. Will you be the woman and dance backwards?", I said, as we joined arms.

"Sure!", he said and we set off on the lower deck (there were no passengers), cannon-ball now singing 'Two lonely people together'. As we danced along, he then sang 'I've got no money for my fare'.

By this time, we were on our way back to the front of the bus and I said to the driver, "Stop the bus and open the doors". After the bus stopped, we danced onto the pavement and I then let go of cannon-ball and nipped smartly back onto the bus, saying, "Drive off!".

The 'Bogeyman' said, "I know that fella".

"Friend of yours?", I enquired.

"No. He's my son-in-law and you were lucky. If you had hit him, he doesn't feel pain."

"Oh yes he does", I replied, "Didn't you the expression on his face as we drove off?"

BOURNEMOUTH TRANSPORT
REGULATIONS and CONDITIONS

GENERAL
(1)   These Regulations and Conditions may be altered without notice.
(2)   Bournemouth Transport will make every effort to maintain the Time Tables as published but alterations may be made without notice. On Bank and Public Holidays, services are liable to alteration or cancellation.
(3)   Bournemouth Transport will not be liable for the stoppage of any service or failure to perform the services, nor will it be liable for any delay, detention or want of punctuality, whether by the default of its servants or agents or otherwise.
(4)   Tickets are not transferable and are issued subject to the Regulations and Conditions published in the Time Tables, Fare Tables and/or Notices of Bournemouth Transport.
(5)   Passengers are not allowed to smoke in the lower saloon of double deck buses.

STANDING PASSENGERS
(6)   Standing passengers will be carried on single deck buses and on the lower deck of double deck buses at any time, except when ascending Richmond Hill. No standing passengers will be carried on the upper deck or staircase of a double deck bus. Standing passengers are not permitted to travel on the platform or steps of any vehicle or standing against the emergency exit or doors or on the gangway forward of the rearmost part of the driver's seat. A maximum of 8 standing passengers will be carried on vehicles with a seating capacity between 24 and 70 and a maximum of 5 standing passengers will be carried on vehicles seating under 24 or over 70.

LOST PROPERTY
(7)   Passengers are carried subject to the provisions of the Public Service Vehicles (Lost Property) Regulations, 1934. Any property found in or upon Bournemouth Transport vehicles must be handed to the Conductor in charge of the vehicle at once. All such property will be deposited at Avenue Road, Bournemouth BH2 5SH, where all enquiries should be made.

PASSENGERS ACCOMPANIED PACKAGES AND LUGGAGE
(8)   All packages and luggage must be accompanied by a fare paying passenger and will be conveyed only at owner's risk. Bournemouth Transport will not accept responsibility for any loss, damage or delay during transit. No packages or luggage over 56lbs. in weight or exceeding a maximum girth measurement of six feet will be accepted on a bus. Bicycles and prams will not be carried.
    Explosives or combustible materials may not be brought on to Bournemouth Transport Public Service Vehicles and will not be conveyed in any circumstances whatever.

DOGS ACCOMPANYING FARE PAYING PASSENGERS
(9)   Dogs are carried only at the discretion of the Conductor and at owner's risk. No large dogs, except Guide Dogs accompanying a blind person, are allowed in or upon Bournemouth Transport buses. A dog taken on the lower deck of a double deck bus or on a single deck bus must be carried on the lap. A dog taken on the upper deck of a double deck bus must be kept on the leash and under control. No charge will be made for Guide Dogs accompanying a blind person, but other dogs will be charged at the child rate, as shown in Bournemouth Transport Fare Tables.

CHILDREN
(10)   One child under five years of age carried free if accompanied by a fare paying passenger or adult pass holder and not occupying a seat. Additional children under five years of age and all children aged 5 to 14 inclusive, carried at the child rate as shown in the fare tables. This rate will also apply to scholars in school uniform up to and including 18 years of age, when travelling to or from school.

PASSENGERS OVER-RIDING
(11)   If a passenger travels beyond the destination paid for, an excess fare will be charged. This will be the fare from the stage to which the passenger paid to the final destination, thus treating the extra distance as a *separate journey*.

SPECIAL FARES AND CHARGES
(12)   Full details of all special fares and charges are shown in the fare tables.

UP A BIT - DOWN A BIT!

The nice thing about working late turns, was that all sorts of characters come out of the woodwork. You never see them in the daytime, which is just as well!

The 'Cisco Kid' was one. He would get on at the Lansdowne stop, dressed in full cowboy outfit, including dummy six-shooters, sit downstairs on the bus and start singing 'The Cattle Call' (for those readers who are not familiar with Country & Western music, Slim Whitman used to sing this song and it became very popular). The song included yodeling and 'Cisco' was good at this, so much so that if a conductor told him to "Shut up!" - or threaten to throw him off the bus - some passengers would turn on the conductor and say, "Leave him alone" and in no time at all, the passengers would be singing with him.

One night, an Inspector boarded my bus and said (or tried to say!), "Have your tickets ready, please". Turning to me, he said, "Do you allow this noise on your bus?".

"I quite like it – everybody goes home happy."

By this time, 'Cisco' had changed his song into 'She'll be coming round the mountain – She'll be wearing big red bloomers' (knickers to younger readers!).

"But not for long", said some passengers. By this time, the whole of the top deck had joined in and the bus sounded like a coach trip returning from Blackpool full of happy trippers.

Everyone was singing, with the exception of the Inspector. "If you don't quieten this bus down, so that I can check the tickets, I'll book you".

"What? For having a noisy bus? If you do, I'm straight down to the *Evening Echo* to give them a story for tomorrow."

The Inspector said, "At least try and make it quieter?".

So, I shouted out, "Can you sing a bit softer, so the Sheriff can check your tickets".

He was not amused! When he had eventually finished checking the tickets and on leaving the bus, his parting shot was, "Booking you! Two overriders upstairs!".

"Good job we didn't have a posse on tonight, then", I quipped.

Those were the fun days. Today, late night buses, one-man-operated, have an air of menace – a bit like the cowboy film 'High Noon'. As for the 'Cisco Kid', he's rode off into the sunset.

As I'm writing this, I recall a recent report from a passenger who rode on the last bus of the evening. It was OMO operated and was a journey to hell! Yobbos swearing; smoking; jumping up and down and ringing the bell; smashing glass and abusing a coloured boy - this would not have happened in my conducting days, I would have had the top deck cleared by the Lansdowne – *passengers ride,* yobbos walk!

Back to my time on the buses, in those days, the front and rear destination screens, for some reason were known as 'blinds'. There were four at the front; stating destination, main points on the route, number of route and whether 'via Old Christchurch Road' or 'Bath Road' or 'Richmond Hill'. Winding the blind on further, you came across: 'To the Cricket' and 'To the Circus' and many a wag left 'To the Circus' showing, via Bath Road and Old Christchurch Road, which caused confusion both to passengers and staff alike!

Many a passenger, seeing the front screen showing 'via Bath Road', got on expecting to get off at the stop on the roundabout by the Royal Bath Hotel, only to find themselves transported via Old Christchurch and outside St. Peter's Church.

Many a time a conductor or driver asked his mate, "Do we go via Bath or Christchurch Road?", discovering too late that he was half-way down the wrong road. At the same time, he would have heard the rapid clattering of feet from passengers on the top deck, all shouting, "You've got Bath Road on the front and you're going down Old Christchurch Road!". The distances between the two roads is not all that great, but if you are late for work, every second counts.

Changing the blinds at all was a work of art and it was particularly easy to forget to change the little blind. To start with, you stood with your arm above your head, peering through a small slit. In the first place, you had to be tall enough to reach the handles and they were always stiff - they never seemed to be have been oiled. After struggling on tip-toe, your arm ached and tempers became frayed, after winding up too far and down too far, to make sure that the screen was within the box.

Short men conductors – and some Clippies – frequently had problems, although if they had a good mate (and if it was not raining), the driver would stand outside the bus, waving his arms up and down, which was a great help. This reminds me of a TV show called the 'Golden Shot'. Contestants had to fire a crossbow at a target and had to rely on their mates telling them 'up a bit' or 'down a bit', 'left a bit' or 'right a bit'!

Blinds on the rear of the bus were frequently forgotten and often a passenger would get on and ask, "Do you go to Christchurch?".

"No!"

"Well, you have Christchurch on the back."

"We've got India on the tyres, but we don't go there either!"

With the advent of one-man-operated buses, the back of the bus was blanked out and often passengers on hearing a bus starting up, would run and say, "Is this a Number 23?".

"No!"

"Well, I wish you would put numbers on the back."

"Then you would know what bus you missed", I used to reply.

Screens could sometimes elicit some funny conversations between Inspectors and crews. One gay Inspector got on my bus and said, "Pull your blinds down".

"Why? What are you going to do with me?"

His reply, "Your front screens only half showing Christchurch – you dizzy queen!" (he always called me that!).

I joked, "Well, we are only going halfway!".

We also had an Inspector called 'Raging Bull'! He was a tall, hefty fella, who always called you 'Mister' (even the women). He used to terrify me. He would rant and rave at you, but as soon as he finished, it would be forgotten. He very rarely reported anybody and used to sort it out on the spot. His pet hate was incorrectly displayed blinds. He used to wait in the Square and if any bus came in showing the wrong blinds, he marched over and tore you off a strip.

Some say he could spot an incorrect blind miles away and one day, he called me on the bus radio when I was five miles away: "Driver Steele, you're showing the wrong number on your front screen".

I radioed back, "Blimey Eric! You've got good eyesight".

Another funny story was when I came into the Square showing the wrong blinds, having changed them at the top of Bath Hill to my next route. You were supposed to wait until you arrived at the Square before changing them and Eric signalled for me to stop, so he could reprimand me. In those days, you could drive into the Square round the roundabout and up the Precinct, then up Old Christchurch Road. Realising I was not going to stop, Eric started chasing me up the Precinct to my stop. For a big man, he had a surprising turn of speed, so much so, that he had actually drawn level with the bus as I reached the stop. As luck would have it, there was nobody waiting at the stop, so I accelerated off, leaving him standing, waving his fist in a big cloud of diesel smoke. My conductor was convulsed with laughter and when he'd finished, he said, "I'm looking forward to our return trip, when you get back in the Square and Raging Bull gets hold of you".

"I'm not going back to the Square, I think I'll report in sick halfway!"

After about 10 minutes, I heard a police car with siren sounding coming up behind the bus. "Blimey! He's out to get you! I bet you wished you stopped in the square and spoke to Eric", said my mate.

When we returned to the Square, Raging Bull was nowhere to be seen. However, another busman walked up to us and said that the story of leaving Eric in a cloud of diesel, had gone all round the canteen (the bus crews' grapevine was better than MI5!). He was still smiling about it and in between fits of laughter, he told us that Raging Bull, in a fit of rage after being left standing in the road, had taken his hat off and thrown it onto the road and another bus had immediately run over it!

We were the heroes of the canteen, but my mate warned, "Keep out of his way for a week and don't come in tomorrow, because when you sign-on in the Square, Eric's going to be looking out for you".

Next day, I ignored his advice and the first person I saw was Eric, who was wearing a new hat! He did not mention the previous day's incident, but when he offered me to help him out, as he put it – overtime for the rest of the week – I hadn't the courage to refuse. He never carried a grudge and as I said, things were quickly forgotten.

How I missed Raging Bull? Those were the days and Inspectors we shall never see again – the world's a little less richer.

LAUGHTER BEST MEDICINE

Now that the days of bus conducting have passed in Bournemouth, a lot of fun at work has gone from life on the buses and the public have lost out as well. Passengers felt safe with a conductor on the bus and they knew help was always at hand.

Take the case of a lady who came down from the upper saloon (they were called saloons, but don't ask me why - there was no bar on board!) although crews usually referred to them as the top deck. The lady said, "Excuse me, conductor. There is a man sitting in the front seat with blood pouring from his mouth".

Now this may surprise you, but bus conductors and drivers were not taught first-aid to help them in the course of their duties. However, in situations like the one described by the lady, you have to act and I ran upstairs and bent over the passenger, who was sat with blood seeping from his mouth. He managed to gasp, "My stomach ulcer's burst".

I ran downstairs and said to my driver, "Find a phone and ring for an ambulance, quick! I'll look after him until it arrives". Back upstairs, the man was almost unconscious and I remembered my wife's comment (she was a Red Cross first-aider), 'never let a person lapsing into unconsciousness, fall asleep'. So, I started telling him jokes (don't ask me why, but it was the only thing that came into my mind).

The ambulance seemed to take ages to arrive and I was running out of jokes, plus you had the bizarre situation of a man bent over with blood coming from his mouth. Anyway, I kept going with, '… here's another funny story …'. With the passengers laughing with me. I managed to keep him awake until the ambulance arrived and judging by the large pool of blood on the floor of the bus, they were just in time.The outcome was that the man made a complete recovery and later thanked me – he even remembered one of my jokes. The Office, after reading my report, asked why I had not been upstairs for two miles to collect the fares! The story soon reached the canteen and I never heard the last of it:

"Your jokes could have finished him off!"

"If I break a leg, don't send for Tommy Steele. The pain will be bad enough!"

I mentioned lack of first-aid training and an incident during my period of training with a senior conductor, could have had serious consequences. A lady, getting on at Christchurch, fell to the floor and started thrashing around. It was a very wet day and she was getting covered in muddy water. I tried to keep her still, but it was very difficult due to her violent convulsions.

The conductor training me, said "Reach in her mouth and take her false teeth out" (you may think this strange first aid!).

However, another passenger said, "Don't do that. She is having an epileptic fit and your fingers could be bitten through". Unknowingly, I had done all that I could have done to stop herself injuring herself.

This was unlike a certain one-man bus driver. A fella got on his bus and asked for the "Lansdowne".

"Forty pence, please."

With that, the fella started banging his head hard on the front windscreen. The driver, sat in his seat watching him, said "I don't know why you are making such a fuss over forty pence!". He had not received any first-aid training and was completely unaware that the man was having an epileptic fit.

On another occasion, working the last Number 6 service of the evening (a notorious one for trouble), when we reached Cunningham Crescent, a fight broke out between two yobbos getting off the bus. One produced a knife, stabbed the other one in the leg, then ran off, leaving just the injured yobbo and myself. The knife had gone through the main artery in the man's leg and my driver, who had qualified as a first-aider before coming on to the buses, knew what he had to do and saved the man's life.

"What's the largest item of lost property you have ever found on your bus?" asked a person in the audience at one of my 'after dinner' speeches recently.

"Six-month old baby in a carrycot!", I replied.

I explained that one day, two young people had got off the bus, looking into each other's eyes. I said, "Have you forgotten something?".

"Oh! *The baby*", they replied.

I said, "Just a minute, I'll have to consult the section on Lost Property in my Rule Book". I read out aloud:

'Conductors must check their bus every time it arrives at a terminus. Any property found should be handed in as soon as possible.'

'If lost property is claimed whilst in your possession and you are satisfied that the claimant is the rightful owner, it must be handed over. The person's name and address must be obtained and entered in the appropriate place on the Lost Property label, which is then handed in at Avenue Road.'

The couple seemed reluctant to give their name and address, but I let them have the baby. I had thought of handing the infant to Bill, the Inspector, but if the baby had started crying, he would have only said "Oh! Me poor 'ead".

It goes without saying, large numbers of gloves are handed in and on a showery day, the Lost Property Office used to fill up with 'orphan' umbrellas.

One driver never bought an umbrella in over 20 years' service. He didn't mind at all the comments from fellow workers on seeing him walking along holding up a dainty ladies' umbrella!

At the end of a day's duty, perishable food did not need to be handed in. One day, I found a large apple pie left on a seat and I said to my mate, "Keep this in your cab until we finish". However, an hour later, a lady got on and said, "Have you found an apple pie on your bus?".

I opened my mouth to say, "Yes", when I noticed my mate behind her, shaking his head violently from side to side. I quickly deduced his intentions, so I replied, "I can't see one".

She got off, saying "I expect somebody picked it up". Then she laughed, "It's gone off. I was taking it back to the shop to complain".

Out of earshot, my mate said, "I've eaten it!".

"What, a whole pie, the size of a dinnerplate?"

I looked at him and he was going green. It was an expensive pie for he was off sick the next day - *without pay.*

One of my most funniest finds, was a blow-up doll. The comments I received walking across Bournemouth Square with it inflated and then handing it in at the Lost Property Office were unbelievable!

If you found a purse, you had to list all the coins, notes and other items which it contained. The last item I found in a purse was a condom (or so I thought), so following procedure, I listed it. Next day, passing the Lost Property Office, I saw Bill the Inspector laughing and waving me to come inside. With his pipe still clenched between his teeth, coughing, he said, "That condom you 'anded in yesterday" … more coughing … "It was a finger-stall!" (a rubber receptacle for a single finger, used for counting paper or bank notes). "Cor blimey! Can't you tell the difference?".

"Well, it fitted *me.*"

"Get im out of ere", he spluttered.

Gagged . . . bus driver Tommy Steele banned from singing on his bus. — Echophoto.

Tommy is silent!

SINGING bus driver Tommy Steele is down in the doldrums after his bosses banned his tuneful melodies when a passenger complained about the noise.

The 52-year-old Southbourne granddad was gagged by a yellow Buses Inspector last week.

"My passengers used to love my singing," said Tommy The Hoot, as he is known by some locals.

"I don't wish to name the Inspector who banned me to save him from embarrassment.

"I sing because I'm happy and enjoy the job. Passengers really enjoy it."

The Inspector told him he must drive the buses, be civil and nothing else, he said.

Tommy, who reckons a traffic warden has the best job in Bournemouth, claims his passengers are compaining that he doesn't sing anymore.

Tommy was most upset because his ban was broadcast over the tannoy system letting passengers know about it.

Tommy, who does a one-hour weekly stint as a disc-jockey for seven local hospitals, has changed the name of his radio programme from "A Handful of Songs" to "A Gagfull of Songs".

Managing director of Yellow Buses, Mr. Ian Cunningham, told the Echo

"This is the first I have heard of it. I do not think personally I would have taken this line.

EVENING ECHO

88th Year — No. 23,372
Monday, March 2, 1987   Price 17p

ROOM FOR ONE ON TOP

Let me take you, dear reader, to the early 1980s, when travelling by bus was a fun period. A good crew working together, could make a bus journey a funny experience. Today, how many times do you have a laugh on a bus? Not many, I bet. Rush here. Rush there. We seem to be going faster and faster and ending up getting nowhere.

I used to look forward to going to work and judging by the amount of overtime I did, I must have lived on a bus! If you can imagine a crowded bus, a smoky atmosphere upstairs and with all the windows shut tight and the conductor and driver shouting out humorous remarks:

"Wipe your feet before you get on! We've just hoovered the bus!"

"Last one on kisses the driver, but knowing my luck, it will be a fella!"

Or, if the queue waiting at a bus stop was slow getting on, instead of "Hurry along please", one driver used to shout, "Come on, break into a walk".

Bus queues were always good for a laugh. Pulling into a stop after heavy snow, I would not let people board until they had shaken the snow off their shoes and it was funny to see a crowd of people dancing up and down before boarding. As you can imagine, the passengers already on board had a good laugh, as did the people getting on!

On a wet day, I would ask people to hang their raincoats in the wardrobe and you'd be surprised to know how many people looked for one, some even going upstairs to see if they could find one!

Pulling into a stop, the queue would sometimes surge forward as people tried to get on, especially if they could see that the bus was already pretty full. A good conductor knew all the stops on a particular route and where there was likely to be a queue. He (or she) would make sure they'd be downstairs, standing by the doors as the bus pulled up. Otherwise, if you were upstairs taking the fares, you'd come down and find ten standing (five being the maximum) and the driver moaning, "I'm not moving this bus 'till some of you get off!".

The standing passengers would look at each other and nobody would move. As the engine of the bus ticked over, you were losing time. This meant that your mate would not get his smoke at the end of the route, because being late, you had to turn round and come straight back.

During the summer, with the heat and large numbers of passengers, a heavy, leather bag full of money cutting into your shoulder, meant that tempers were likely to become frayed. One day, I remember we pulled into a stop too fast and the fella, standing at the front of the queue, had his wig blown off! "Room for one on top", I shouted.

A good conductor would also know how many seats were available and I say 'good', because you were either collecting fares, looking out for passengers over-riding and dashing up and down stairs.

When you pulled into a stop, the queue would very often surge forward and you would then put your arm across the door, shouting, "Let them off first, please". Then followed a scene similar to a rugby scrum, with the passengers trying to force their way on and passengers trying to force their way off, the tired, hot and sweat-soaked conductor in the middle. Having managed to clear the platform of passengers getting off, you would shout, "First four, please". After counting four, you would say, "That's it. Full right up".

The British are the best people in the world when it comes to queuing and most people would accept the bus was full, but a few would look at you with pleading eyes (similar to my dog when I'm not taking him for a walk). Others, with short tempers, would shout, "I've been waiting for you for half-an-hour!".

"That's nothing. My mother waited nine months for me!"

"Let me on, there'll be somebody getting off at the next stop."

"Yes, me!", I would reply.

On one occasion, having counted my required number of passengers, I put my arm across and said, "Sorry. Full up".

A lady turned to me and said, "That's my daughter you've just stopped getting on, You wouldn't separate a mother from her daughter, would you?".

"No Love. I did that 25 years ago and I've regretted it ever since."

One lady got on, who was no oil painting, more an 'old master', saying, "Don't let that man on behind me. He's been making suggestive remarks and touching me". The man in question was a short, skinny little man with a hangdog expression and drooping moustache. Head bowed, he got on with a Jack Russell dog tied to a piece of string.

Remember, in those days the buses were 'front loaders', with the doors at the front. My driver that day happened to be Neil, who was always sarcastic. He said, "I should kick his blind dog, luv!". Then he said in my ear, "She looks like that woman Mandy (from the Dick Emery Show), you know, the man-hungry one!".

"Oh! You are awful, but I like you", I replied. I wouldn't swear to it, but I thought I saw the shadow of a thin smile from Neil.

During the 1980s, personal shopping trolleys were more in fashion and bus companies should have run courses on how to lift them, filled with a week's shopping onto the bus, correctly. Many a conductor, after trying to lift one using the one-hand technique, had to sign-off sick with a bad back (or if it was a weekend coming up, so they said). A lot of conductors refused to lift them and would conveniently be upstairs if they spotted somebody waiting with a trolley at the bus stop.

Helping mums on with their pushchairs was another duty conductors performed. One summer day, a mother with three young children standing at the bus stop, asked me to help her on with her luggage. After helping her and the children on, I then loaded the cases into the luggage space.

I was just about to ring the bell, when I felt a tap on my shoulder with a newspaper. "Don't forget the pram by the wall", said a fella.

"Who are you?", I asked.

"'E's me husband", she replied.

"Well, why don't you bring the pram on?"

"I'm on holiday", he replied.

I remembered that old radio show 'Ignorance is Bliss 'tis Folly to be Wise'.

Helping passengers on and off the bus was common, although some yobbos and drunks complained after the toe of the conductor's boot speeded up their departure! Eighteen-year-old blondes had the best chance of a helping hand, but mostly it was senior citizens that required a lift.

However, you had to be careful. Some people pushed your hand away saying, "Leave me alone. I can get on by myself".

Grabbing the wrist of one lady who was slow getting on, with a mighty heave, I lifted her onto the platform, where she collapsed, holding her wrist saying, "I broke my wrist a few weeks ago, now you gone and broken it again". Concerned, I offered to call an ambulance, which she declined.

Meanwhile, my driver Gordon, who was gay and had the nickname Gay Gordon said, "Well, he wasn't to know, luv. Sit down and by the way, I don't like your hat – it doesn't match your dress!".

Helping a nineteen-stone lady off the bus one day, sent my driver Ken's temperature into overdrive. It was a very hot, summer's day. We were running late (with a bus sitting behind, refusing to overtake, despite Ken waving him past) and we were doing all the work. Ken liked his cup of tea at Tuckton Bridge and running late would mean turning straight round and coming back without a break, to try and keep to the timetable.

This lady got on at Derby Road and I had to spend some time lifting, pushing and shoving her on board. After two stops, she stood up to get off and once more, this time with the assistance of another passenger, we had to manoeuvre her off (Ken would not assist and he sat in the driver's seat with a face like thunder, looking at his watch). Anyway, after a bit of 'leg up a bit – down a bit', we eventually got her off and onto the pavement.

Ken was just about to close the door, when he said to the poor woman (a bit sarcastically) and through clenched teeth, "Alright now?".

"This is Boscombe Arcade shops?", she asked.

"No! It's *Boscombe Gardens*", shouted Ken.

"Oh! I thought I couldn't see any shops", she said, getting back onto the bus. *Ken exploded!*

"It's your fault" she said. "You should shout out the name of the stops."

"And you should go on a diet", shouted Ken back.

Of course, shouting out the name of the fare stage stops was all part of the duty of a conductor. This was alright when you had a half-full bus, but in the summer with a full load, it took you all your time to collect the fares.

One conductor got into trouble by shouting out 'Derby Road', but adding 'Red light district of Bournemouth!'.

I would make jokes like, "Seamoor Road. Change here for the nudist colony!". Would you believe it, one fella (in a raincoat) asked me where it was? I pointed to a house with a high fence around it and said, "Over the road". The last I saw of him, he was peeping through a hole in the fence.

Several routes starting in the Square, went through Boscombe and I used to think the whole of the holidaymakers stayed there. While the bus was waiting in the Square, they would come up and ask, "Do you go to Boscombe?".

"Yes", you would say several hundred times a day. In the end, I made up a big white card, with the words 'YES! WE GO TO BOSCOMBE' printed on it.

Sometimes, if you were standing with your back to them, they would come up and tap you on the shoulder and begin, "Do you ...?". I would then turn round and they would see the card, "Oooh! Thanks".

PASSENGER TRAINING SCHOOL

Stepping onto my bus, I looked at my driver for the week and I immediately knew I was going to enjoy working with him. Some people almost smile with their eyes and not only that, his eyes were mischievous (my dictionary informs me that the word mischievous means 'inclined to annoy with playful tricks').

This driver was only one of a handful of people that have played a trick on me, although a lot have tried, including the television personality Noel Edmunds (who failed).

Sadly, this driver was involved in a tragic accident, from which he never recovered and he was never the same man again.

His nickname was 'Steve the Fish'. He got this nickname, not because he was a fisherman (never been fishing in his life), but he always had a plastic fish sticking out of his top pocket while driving a bus and he even dressed the fish in different hats. One day, he came in work with a scarf tied round the fish's neck. "It's got a cold", he explained.

In those days, it was the custom for conductors to nip off the bus and purchase cakes, cans of soft drinks, bags of crisps and so on. One day, pulling up outside a butcher's shop, Steve said, "Pop in and get us a pork pie – I'll give you the money when you come back".

"Large or small?"

"Large, I'm hungry!"

Running into the shop, I said, "Large pork pie, please".

The butcher looked at me and the bus ticking over outside and said, "Is that the twit with the fish sticking out of his pocket driving the bus?"

"Yes. How did you know?"

"Because that twit keeps sending conductors in here for pork pies."

"What's wrong with that?"

"Nothing, except that we are a kosher butcher!"

Another duty of the conductor was 'putting the tea bag in'. In the gardens, just off Gervis Place in the Square at Bournemouth, was a little hut. We used to call it 'Snake'ees', but don't ask me why? Inside the hut was a hot water urn, a sink and a wooden seat. On the wall, somebody had written 'I'm a mushroom. They keep me in the dark and feed me bulls**t'.

The place stank, which was hardly surprising, when you consider it was the home of a well-known local tramp, called 'Smelly' (he was always being evicted for some of the unmentionable things he used the sink for!).

The hot water from the urn always made the best tea I have ever tasted and conductors would fill a vacuum flask of hot water to take with them at the start of the journey. When the bus reached Boscombe Arcade, the driver would say, "Put the tea bag in" and by the time the bus reached Hengistbury Head, the tea would be brewed. Unlike today's rush and tear on today's one-man–operated buses, you had ten minutes (if you worked it right) to enjoy the brew before having to start the return journey.

Steve loved his tea and kept the doors at the front of the bus shut, to prevent passengers boarding. "Right! Pour it out", said Steve, rubbing his hands together.

"No. You pour it out, Steve." Reaching for the flask, he went to pour the brew into a cup. However, much to his surprise, out fell a tea bag – no water! The look on his face had to be seen to be believed. I said, "You said put the tea bag in - nothing about water! Tell you what, how about a pork pie instead?". *We were even.*

Halfway through our week together, we decided to start a Passengers' Training School. This is how it worked. Passengers would get on and Steve, sitting in the driver's seat, would welcome them aboard. "Good morning, ladies and gentlemen and any others that followed you aboard. This morning, my conductor Tommy Steele, will be conducting a Passengers' Training School. Please, take your seats, so that we can get started".

Going around the bus, collecting the fares, I would explain, "Today I shall cover the basic rules of becoming a good passenger. Remember, I'm here to help you enjoy your journey, so please help me by having the correct fare ready and stating your destination. Over to you, Steve".

Steve said, "Please give adequate notice of your intention to alight from this bus by ringing the bell once, *not* several times, as it's confusing. Please remember to say 'Thank You, driver, I really enjoyed my journey. If you have not enjoyed the journey, *say nothing!* Over to you, Tom".

I continued, "if you can avoid going upstairs, please do so, because by sitting downstairs, you are helping my legs – I get very tired going up and down stairs all day, so tired, in fact, that I'm thinking of moving from my house into a bungalow".

One day, Steve hung a roll of tickets across the bottom rails of the staircase and made up a sign 'Out of Order'. Anybody getting on would be asked to sit downstairs. We even had an Inspector get on and ask why the stairs were blanked off? Steve's quick thinking saved us, "Someone's been sick at the top of the stairs".

"Well, you should have a bus change - you can't have 15 standing downstairs!"

We would tell people, that after attending our Passenger Training School, we would select a passenger, to go through, all expenses paid, to the final in London of 'The Passenger of the Year Competition'. You would be surprised to know just how many people did not go upstairs; had the correct money ready and rang the bell in time to get off at their stop.

I worked with Steve many times, even changing with the conductor who had been booked to work with him. You were allowed to change duties with another conductor, providing you informed the Traffic Office and providing the duty you had to offer was a good one (the hours on some duties were not popular).

Have you ever said something that you regretted later? One day I met Steve who was coming off duty. I said, "Had a good day, Steve?".

"No", he said and walked on, looking very sad. Later in the canteen, somebody told me that Steve had been working a one-man-operated bus, when it had been involved in an accident, a senior citizen's leg having gone under the rear wheel of the bus. The person died three weeks later.

I should explain here that if a driver was involved in an accident, where death or serious injury occurred, the driver was made to drive an empty bus as soon as possible afterwards. The reason for doing this, was that shock could result in a driver not driving again, even if the accident was not the fault of the driver, which was the situation in many cases.

I would like to add here that in all my years bus and coach driving, considering the millions of journeys undertaken by bus and coach drivers, very very few accidents were the fault of the bus or coach driver. So, rest assured, you are extremely safe on buses and coaches.

Tommy sings for joy now

HAPPY-GO-LUCKY bus driver Tommy Steele was singing for joy after Yellow Buses gave his sing-a-long roadshow the thumbs up.

Cheery granddad Tommy (52) told how he had been barred from bursting into song by a "spoilsport" inspector after his drive-a-long ditties came over his intercom by mistake.

The Echo's story made him a celebrity overnight!

"People recognise me when I go shopping — the Echo has made me famous!" beamed "Tommy The Hoot" as he's known around Southbourne where he lives.

Aptly enough, his favourite hit is "Iv'e Got A Handful of Songs To Sing You" by his famous name-sake — he plays the star's records on local hospitals' Radio Bedside where he is a DJ.

But his wife Valerie has mixed views about Tommy's tunes — she reckons he's tone deaf!

"She has suffered my singing for 30 years, she deserves a medal!" joked Tommy.

Yellow Buses general manager Mr. Ian Cunningham confirmed it was okay for Tommy to sing but he said he had been told to "use his discretion."

WE SAY

EVENING ECHO

TUESDAY MARCH 3 1987

News: 24601
Tel.Ads: 295555
RICHMOND HILL, BOURNEMOUTH

Out of tune

TOMMY STEELE — or Tommy the Hoot to his friends — was ordered by an unnamed inspector last week to cease the vocal renditions, drive the buses, be civil and nothing else. A passenger (just one) had complained.

"I sing because I'm happy," says Tommy. "Passengers really enjoy it."

Since the gagging, many of them have been complaining of silence . . . and Mr. Ian Cunningham, managing director of Yellow Buses, told our reporter: "This is the first I have heard of it. I do not think personally I would have taken this line."

With a bit of luck and some enlightened management, Tommy will be back on song before long — and perhaps the passenger who didn't like to hear job satisfaction expressed so tunefully should wait for the next bus!

56

CLEAN ROUND
THE ROUNDABOUT

"Wimborne Willy gone sick", said the Inspector.

"Thank Goodness for that! I don't want him ill, but I wasn't looking forward to working with him", I replied.

'Wimborne Willy' had the reputation of being a rough driver and some people will never make good drivers, their bodies not having the rhythm.

In the case of 'Wimborne', it was his right foot that never had rhythm! For a start, he wore size 12 boots and when stopping a bus, instead of 'feathering' the brake and slowing the bus down gently, he trod on the pedal.

Now, bus brakes are good; they have to be when you consider how much weight they have to bring to a halt. If you gradually put pressure on the brake pedal, the bus will gradually stop. Put it on hard and everybody joins the driver in the cab, well, not quite, but it stops with a jerk. Imagine the number of bus stops you pull into during an eight-hour shift, not to mention braking in traffic.

Now, the conductor has to brace himself every time the bus comes to a halt and it soon becomes an art. You quickly sense when the bus is going to stop and you brace yourself automatically. If you have a good driver who is smooth, you hardly notice you are doing it, but if you have a rough driver, using heavy braking, you are already bracing yourself before he stops and elderly passengers, standing up, have to cling onto the hand-rails, like a sailor in a force-10 gale. The result of all this heavy braking is that the poor conductor's legs soon begin to ache, followed by his back and that was why I was pleased when 'Wimborne Willy' went sick.

The last I heard of 'Wimborne' was that he was driving a tour bus round London. With the density of traffic there, the tourists must have been singing 'All Shook Up' as they saw the sights!

My joy of losing 'Wimborne' was cut short when I found out my driver was to be 'Flash Mickey', one of the fastest drivers on Bournemouth Transport at the time. I had exchanged one bracing driver for another. He could get a bus through traffic like a snake going through long grass and if the Traffic Office could have used Mickey to compose the timetable, they'd have only needed half the buses.

Quick journeys meant less passengers to take fares from and more time spent at the terminus drinking tea. The fact that a dear old lady had come out to catch the 4.20p.m. Number 23, which, because of Mickey's driving, had left her stop at 4.16p.m. and which meant that she had another half-an-hour to wait for the next bus, didn't bother Mickey, as he prided himself on being the fastest driver.

Sometime previously, a conductor warned me, "Look out, or he'll have you over". I hadn't taken much notice at the time of what he had said, but today, I was to find out what he meant!

I was on the top deck of a crowded bus, taking the fares and aware that Mickey was weaving in and out of the traffic, as was his normal fashion. Suddenly, he swerved to avoid a car. Caught off balance, I landed flat on my back and to this day, I can picture the scene of looking up a delightful young lady's skirt, while hearing all the money from my cash bag rolling around the floor!

Pandemonium broke out, with passengers shouting out, "Stop the bus, driver!". Meanwhile, the young lady was trying to pull her skirt tighter round her knees. I got up and saw that my nice, clean uniform was covered in dust.

My first concern, of course, was the money. Some of the passengers helped, picking up piles of change and handing it to me and at the end of the day when I cashed up, I found that I actually had more cash than my waybill indicated I should have!

Mickey, meanwhile, sat in the driver's seat and when I came down the stairs, he called out, "Alright?" and accelerated away. If I had gone sick or written a report about the accident, I could have got Mickey into a lot of trouble. The Office knew he was a mad driver, because of the amount of merit bonus he had been stopped in the past and complaints made by other conductors. However, they had never taken any action against him, because so far, he had not injured a passenger and because they were short of drivers. In one way, I wish I had reported him, because for weeks after, he went round telling people, "I've had Tommy Steele over!".

However, there's a twist to this story. Every year, Yellow Buses took part in a national competition to find the 'Bus Driver of the Year'. This consisted of a series of tests at Mallard Road Depot, held once a year on a Sunday, when drivers were put through their paces. You had to manoeuvre a bus through a series of traffic cones, (not easy when your front wheels are set back from the front of the bus, in fact, behind the driver's seat) and another test was stopping the bus within a given distance. Winners of the heat went on to the final held in Blackpool, which consisted of advanced tests, the winner becoming 'Bus Driver of the Year'. One thing I would say about Mickey, he could handle a bus and one year, much to everybody's surprise, he won the event.

Some time later, he was caught in a police speed trap and fined. He had been doing over 30 miles an hour, driving an empty bus back to Bournemouth from Wareham! This was hot news in the canteen and Mickey's pride was dented. However, on the plus side, he had been caught speeding and as one wag said in the canteen, "If he's 'Bus Driver of the Year', what's the rest of them like?".

'Blind Eddie' was another driver who gave a rough ride, so that when you were with him, you always followed the golden rule 'hold on with one hand at all times'. Eddie acquired his nickname because his eyes were permanently half-shut! He once gave me a lift home in his car, going at over 70 miles-an-hour most of the way and only slowing down when I asked him if he was trying to get airborne?

Eddie's one ambition in life was to become a millionaire and he would spend hours doing the football pools and studying stocks and shares. This became such an obsession with him that he would point out any rich person in a newspaper and say, "Lord, why not me?". I used to upset him by going round the bus, singing 'If I Was a Rich Man'. One day, I kidded him that one particular passenger was a millionaire and as this person alighted, Eddie burst out with, "What are *you* travelling by bus for?".

"I beg your pardon!"

"With all your money, why are you travelling by bus", repeated Eddie.

"How do *you* know how much money I have?", said the passenger, looking at me quizzically.

I made a sign to him indicating that Eddie was 'not all there' and the passenger finished getting off, muttering under his breath, "Strange fellow!".

Eddie shouting after him, said, "Next time, travel in your Rolls". The passenger must have thought that Yellow Bus drivers were indeed strange fellows.

Another 'strange' fellow was 'Harpic', so named because of a well-known cleaning product for toilets, which had an advertising slogan 'Clean Round the Bend'. Harpic's driving was not so much rough, but 'going round in circles'. He could not resist going round roundabouts, twice or even sometimes *three* times, shouting as he did so, "Look at the flowers". The passengers would have done so, if they could, but they were too giddy!

I would call out, "Were you born in a fairground?".

"What do you mean?"

"Were you born on a roundabout?"

The Office learned about Harpic's strange behaviour after an Inspector, checking tickets on his bus, failed to realise that after holding on while the bus went round the roundabout once, that he was going round again! He lost his balance and ended up, clinging on for dear life and with his arms round a lady's neck, while Harpic shouted, "Look at the flowers". The Inspector, after unravelling himself from a surprised lady and then picking up his hat from the floor, was in no mood to look at the flowers. Instead, he shouted out, "You! Look at the road!".

Harpic caught me out in the same way at the start of a journey from Bournemouth. In those days, you used to start out from Gervis Place and then go round the roundabout, past W. H. Smith's and up Old Christchurch Road. We started off OK and I started taking fares, unaware that Harpic was going round again.

It was a hot summer's day and using both hands to wind the tickets off, I was off balance and ended up being propelled backwards, ending up sitting on a very surprised lady's lap. This would have been alright, had it not been for the fact that the lady had a cream cake in a box resting on her lap. Cream cakes are not designed to have 12-stone bus conductors sat on top of them and in a flash, it became a cream sandwich! I still remember the lady's screams and above them a voice shouting, "Look at the flowers".

Another time, I finished up with a man entangled around me on the floor after again being caught off guard. On a further occasion, I grabbed what I thought was the handrail, only to find that it was passenger standing-up holding a long broom handle. Caught off-balance, I pulled both handle and passenger down on top of myself onto the floor of the bus.

At the end of this particular journey, Harpic said, "Would you like a hot drink?".

"Yes please" and he poured one out from his flask. I took a sip and pulled a face.

"What's the matter?"

"This drink tastes funny."

"Oh, that. Well, it's coffee and tea mixed up together. When I got up this morning, I couldn't make up my mind if I wanted tea or coffee, so I made both."

"In the same flask?"

"Well, I haven't got two."

As I've said before, Bournemouth Transport was short of drivers, even if journeys did take twice as long!

60

SILLY SEASON

'Summer season and I'm appearing in Bournemouth', was a joke I used to use with the passengers (readers will recall that I used to be a comedian).

One day, an old lady passenger said to me, "Why did you give up being a comedian?".

"Couldn't stand the audience throwing tomatoes at me!"

"They did that? How terrible."

"Wouldn't have been so bad if they'd taken them out of the tins first!"

She looked at me, with a serious face, not laughing.

I continued, "I once did a mime act and the audience mimed laughter."

"Goodness me! You *have* suffered."

"Not half as much as his audience", quipped my mate. "It's his singing I can't stand. First thing in the morning, he's shouting out, 'Come on Butler, get this bus out'". A reference, of course, to the popular TV series 'On the Buses', although I can assure readers, that what actually happens in real life 'on the buses', is far funnier, as my books will reveal.

The Inspector who was on the bus at the time, said to the passengers, "You haven't been listening to these two idiots?".

I said, "We're only *acting* like idiots, although some of the staff aren't!".

The passengers then joined in, one shouting out "Like Blakey!" and the Inspector shot him a black look. At the time, the TV programme 'On the Buses' had been running for several weeks and turned all bus Inspectors throughout the country into 'Blakeys'. Some were getting a bit fed up with it and one Bournemouth Inspector had even booked a driver who refused to stop calling him Blakey.

One of the passengers called out, "Wish we had your conductor in Southend".

"So do I! *Now get this bus going.*"

As we roared away, I started going round the bus collecting fares. "Are you and your mate always like this?", asked a passenger.

I replied, "When we work together, we always have a good laugh - it makes the shift go quicker". I should explain, in bus work, you never asked, 'How long have you got left on your turn?'. It was, 'How many have you got left to do?'. The answer would be, 'I've got a twenty three and a twenty'. 'Nip into the hut, there's plenty of overtime', would be the reply. The answer would be unprintable!

Going on round the bus, the passengers were still laughing. One said, "Better than the Summer Show we went to last night. The comic was rubbish. I tell you, he couldn't have made my granny laugh! I say, he couldn't have made my granny laugh" (repeating himself).

"Why not?" I asked.

"Cos she's dead!" The bus roared …

On this occasion, it took me twice as long to go round the bus collecting the rest of the fares. The passengers kept stopping me: "Ere, have you 'eard this one?". Yes, those were the days. Try raising a laugh on a one-man-operated bus today?

The lady with the serious expression on her face, had still not finished with me. As she waited to get off at her stop, she said to me, "Conductor. When you were on the stage performing, how good a comedian were you?".

"Shows you how good I was, lady. I'm conducting a bus now."

Still without a smile on her face, all she could say as she walked away, was "Oh!".

"I've had audiences like her", I said to the remaining passengers. "I once played to an undertaker's convention and half-way through the act, I told them all to join hands, the last one having to wet his finger and stick it into the light socket!".

More roars of laughter – "We'll look out for *you* again".

Bus crews nicknamed the summer service, the 'silly season'. Bournemouth being a holiday town, received a large number of holidaymakers and they asked lots of questions. Personally, I realised that these were people who were in a strange town, who didn't know their way round and I did my best to help them. Some of my mates, however, being a bit short-tempered, ignored their questions, or gave them a short, snappy answer.

For some reason, bare feet on buses upset some conductors, resulting in conversations such as, "You're not getting on *my* bus with bare feet".

"Well, I can't leave them at the bus stop while I go home."

"Leave them where you like, but not on *my* bus."

"Why can't I travel with bare feet?"

"Because you could tread on a lighted cigarette upstairs."

"If I promise to avoid cigarette ends and sit downstairs, will it be alright?"

"No!"

"Show me in your Rule Book where it says passengers cannot travel in bare feet."

"Look! Shoes on, or your *off*!" This conversation shows you how silly arguments started in the summer.

If you were working main road routes 20, 21, 22 and 23, which all went through Boscombe, you would have a stream of people asking, as they got on the bus, such as, "Do you go to Boscombe?". Sometimes they received replies they didn't expect!

"What's it got on the front?"

"Errr, I didn't look."

"Do you always get on a bus without looking to see where it's going? Where you from?"

"Bradford."

"Beats me how you found your way to Bournemouth, or, how you're getting back?"

"There's no need to be rude. I was only asking a civil question."

"Yeah! You and forty-thousand others! Do you know how many times I'm asked 'Do you go to Boscombe?'."

"Well, I thought you were here to help the public?"

"Look mate. I spend a lot of time winding the handles on the route indicators on the front of the bus, putting up 'Boscombe' to help the public."

Winding the handles to change the destination blinds could be a bind on a hot summer's day. To start with, you only had a slit to peer through to see if you had put the right destination up and it reminded me of looking through a periscope. Sometimes, you would wind the wrong way and have to wind back again. The handles were stiff and hard to turn. Looking up, perspiration would run into your eyes. The heavy 'setright' ticket machine would cut into your shoulders through your thin, summer shirt and many times during the summer months, I had red wheals all over my shoulders.

All this, plus if you were working main roads, you were busy the whole time with hardly anytime for tea breaks or smokes between routes. That's why one day, when Ken my short-tempered driver, had made five minutes to have a cup of tea at Tuckton Bridge terminus, he blew his top!

When you get to the end of your route, all you want is to enjoy a quiet rest. So, you keep the doors of the bus shut and go upstairs to get away from the pleading expressions of people waiting to board. When it's raining, it's even worse, people banging on the door to be let on board and although it may seem cruel, you really do need peace and quiet at the end of a hectic trip.

This one had been particularly hectic and Ken, who was operating the doors at the front of the bus, had shut an alighting passenger's leg in the door!

"You want to be a bit more careful!", shouted the irate passenger, as he limped off.

Ken shouted back, " And you want to move a bit quicker".

Ken had a habit of shutting passengers in the door and the day before, after a lady had boarded, he shut the doors quick and started to drive off.

The woman said, "Stop!".

"Can't stop between stops", Ken had replied.

"My husband was behind me waiting to get on and you shut the doors in his face." Ken was unmoved and at the next stop he let her off to walk back to find her husband.

When something like this happens, it can create a bit of an atmosphere with the other passengers and you are not working as a crew. To ease the tension, I joked, "Ken, you should never come between a man and his wife". Anyway, at the end of the journey, we settled down for a nice up of tea.

Ken was really a very kind man, who gave most of his wages to help sick horses (mind you, he didn't know they were sick when he placed bets on them!). After working with him for a few days, I realised that when his head was inside the newspaper, like it was now, engrossed with the racing page, you left him alone – he wouldn't answer anyway.

Suddenly, two women got on the bus and I heard, "Do you go to Boscombe?". Ken looked at me. "Did you forget to shut the doors?"

"Looks like it", I said and Ken's head went back inside his paper.

"Do you go to Boscombe?", the lady called out again and I had to say 'Yes', because we had 'Boscombe' on the front.

Some crews used to blank off the screens, or put up 'Reserved' when they were having their break. You'd be surprised to know that, sometimes when a conductor had forgotten to change the blind on the front of the bus, so that it was still displaying 'Reserved', how many ordinary passengers would climb on board when the bus stopped.

On this occasion, because it was a short break, the two ladies after boarding, sat behind Ken. "Nice day, driver", said one. No reply.

"How far is it to Boscombe?" I could see Ken getting agitated.

"You're lucky working in a seaside town."

"Have you been working here long?"

Ken stood up. "Too bloody long! Why don't you shut-up? Stop Talking. Give a man some peace."

The ladies were taken aback. "No need to be rude. You should be polite to your passengers."

Ken was now shaking with rage. "This job would be alright if we didn't have to stop and pick up *passengers*." With that, he screwed his newspaper up into a ball and threw it at them - such was his temper and aim, that it missed! He then stormed off the bus.

"Well, I've never been spoken to that in all my life", said one of the ladies.

To calm the situation down, I joked, "Take no notice of him. His wife's run off with an Inspector and he's going to miss him".

Ken eventually came back to the bus, climbed into the driver's seat and drove off. When the ladies got off at Boscombe, one called out, "Hope your wife comes back".

"It's not his wife, it's the Inspector", I shouted after them.

After that incident, I always made sure that the doors were closed when we had our tea breaks.

TOMMY'S TICKLER!

Recently, a bus driver was given the job of transferring some patients from one mental hospital to another. Shortly after collecting his passengers, the driver was caught short. Not being able to wait any longer, he decided to answer the call of nature by calling at a public house along his route, leaving his passengers in the bus.

He was gone only a few minutes, but when he returned he found the bus empty and no sign of his passengers. He knew he would be in serious trouble with the mental hospital for losing them, but nonetheless, he decided to continue with his journey.

It was a mainly rural area and buses were few and far between. So, coming across a large group of people waiting at a bus stop, he pulled in, the group being more than pleased to accept a lift.

With that, he closed the doors and didn't stop until he reached the mental hospital, who were very pleased to receive the patients they had been expecting.

TOMMY'S TICKLERS!

Conductor gets into an argument over the correct fare with a passenger. The passenger ends up shoving a pound coin up the conductor's nose. The conductor gets taken to hospital to have the coin removed and is kept in for observation. The bus company rings up and to ask the hospital how he is? "No change", comes the answer.

It was a busy time for the ticket clerk writing out tickets to various destinations. The other clerk was on holiday and the queue was building up.
The next customer was a man in his thirties, not too tidy and a couple of day's growth of beard. He had a newspaper in his hand and asked, "Could I have a ticket to Jeopardy, please?".
"Is that Jeopardy with a G or a J"?, asked the clerk, who was obviously under some pressure.
The unkempt man referred to his newspaper and said, "It's with a J".
After some time studying her 'A-Z of Destinations', the clerk looked up and said, Well, I can't find it. What part of the country is it in?".
"I'm not sure", replied the man, "But it's here in the paper" and he lifted it up to show, '1,000 JOBS IN JEOPARDY', "and I'd like to get one", he said.

"Excuse me, conductor. How long will the next bus be?"
"Thirty-nine feet, luv, same as this one."
"Will it have a monkey on it collecting the fares, the same as this one?"
"No luv. We carry them, we don't employ them!"

OVER AND OUT

Some people get through life by living on their wits and my driver nicknamed 'The Artful Dodger' was one. We were running empty from Mallard Road Depot to pick up our route from outside the Civic Offices - Christchurch (Route 21) to Bournemouth Square.

"How are you getting on with the job?"

"Alright. I enjoy working with people and I've lost weight running up and down stairs."

"Public are a lot of tossers! I wouldn't give you tuppence for them." He continued, "You take the other day. I waited for a runner (I should explain that the term 'runner' was given to anybody running for a bus) and what happens? She reports me fer running early!".

"And were yuh running early?"

"Yea!" He continued, "I'm only on this job 'til something better comes up."

"Like most of the others", I replied, "But, what's *something better*?".

"Well, a nice little factory job, five day week, with Saturday and Sunday off. I hate working Saturday nights, should be out wiv me mates having a good time."

Saturday night was the most popular night for staff ringing in sick (unless Bournemouth Football Club was playing at home on a Saturday afternoon, then the sickness rate for the afternoon went up!).

One driver who reported sick, went to go to an afternoon match, but arrived late and missed the kick-off, because the bus he should have caught didn't run. He later found out that this would have been the service he should have been driving, if he hadn't reported sick!

During the day, the 'Artful Dodger' lived up to his nickname. On busy routes, you could hang back in the distance and let the bus in front do all the work. However, at the end of the route, you would overtake him and pick up the few passengers left at stops, which meant that you had more time for tea and a smoke at the end of your route.

A smoke was very important to some crews and got them through the day, especially during the Summer when things were very busy. Nowadays, you watch a one-man bus driver having a smoke (if he has the time?). The stress is such that it's like watching a condemned man about to face a firing squad.

Another one of Dodger's tricks, was if several bus routes stopped at one stop and a bus was already on the stop, he would overtake, pretending not to see the people running out, putting their hands out for him to stop.

I should say at this point, that a lot of people in Bournemouth only put their hands out to signal the bus to stop, when they realised – too late – that the bus was not stopping. Also and unfortunately for anybody trying to get on, when you were approaching a stop with a full load and made to go past, a quick hand stuck out and a look of sorrow would not change the driver's mind. The Dodger would not stop sometimes, even if he did not have a full load, completely ignoring the fists (and other gestures!) being waved at him.

Another trick was to miss out part of the route. One day, a startled passenger jumped up and said to Dodger, "Driver, doesn't this bus go down the Broadway?".

"Not this one luv, you want the one behind."

"But, I swear this one went down the Broadway on Monday!"

"You shouldn't swear, luv."

"You would if you had to walk down that long road carrying two bags of shopping. I'm going to find out about this."

"I shouldn't bother luv, they've changed the timetable since yesterday."

"No! They've changed the driver – I'm going to report you."

"Please yourself luv, but you won't meet a better driver than me."

I did feel sorry for her having to walk down a long road, carrying her shopping. Dodger was unmoved and I said to him, "That wasn't very nice".

Surprised, he looked at me and said, "Do you want a longer tea break at the end?".

"Yes, but not by treating the passengers like that."

"Tossers, all of them."

"If you carry on like that, you'll get the sack."

"Couldn't give a monkey, mate. If they sack me, I'll be down the Labour Exchange, sign on and lay on the beach all day."

"If that lady rings up, you'll lose your merit bonus."

"Couldn't give a toss! I've already loss this six month's money and part of the next, but I gets it back off the Company."

"How?"

"I'll show you later, if we get one of the older buses."

I should explain, we lived at the time in an era which made the Prime Minister at that time say, "You have never had it so good". There were plenty of jobs around and once you signed-on at the Labour Exchange and if you did not want to work, you could lay on the beach all day.

Dodger was a single man and did some moonlighting window cleaning. At the time, it was said that the bus companies could not get workers 'for love nor money', which was true. Not many people wanted to work on the buses, with shift working, poor pay - the reason for poor pay being if you were paid more money, the fares would have to go up - so many family men had to work hours of overtime to bring in a decent wage.

The shortage of bus workers also meant deteriorating standards. In the old days, busmen were always smartly dressed, having to wear collar and tie, as well as a heavy hat, even during very hot weather. A lot of pride was taken in the job and the public received good service. When I joined, standards were already slipping, despite the Inspectors doing their best to keep both service and dress up to scratch. However, a lot of the younger men who joined, couldn't care less and if any of the older Inspectors reprimanded them, they would say, "We're not in the old trolley bus days, grandad!".

One day in the canteen, a driver told me about an Inspector who had got on his bus to check him for wearing a brightly coloured shirt. He described the Inspector as being bald, but he was also a bit of a ladies man and sometimes he used to wear a grey wig to cover up his baldness. Apparently, on an earlier occasion, he had got on a bus and the conductor had said, 'Blimey! What's that squirrel doing on your head?'. The tale had gone round the canteen like wildfire, resulting in the Inspector earning the nickname, the 'Squirrel'.

The driver told me that the 'Squirrel' had got on his bus and said, "Why are you wearing that orange shirt, instead of your blue uniform shirt?".

"It's in the wash, right?"

"Where's your other shirts?"

"In the airing cupboard."

"Well, you can't drive a bus wearing an orange shirt."

The driver said that he had then stopped the bus, took his shirt off and "*OK*?".

"You can't drive a bus stripped to the waist."

"OK, you drive it" and he stopped the bus and got off (Inspectors were not allowed to drive buses in service).

The Inspector said, "Get back on and get your blue shirts out of the airing cupboard tomorrow".

Amazingly, he didn't get the sack, but in those days, if you'd murdered somebody and got a suspended sentence, you would still have been allowed to drive a bus. The Inspector may well have lost face, but would have bided his time and, no doubt, catch the driver running early at a later date and I don't think the driver would have boasted about that in the canteen!

BOURNEMOUTH TRANSPORT

H A N D B O O K
OF
REGULATIONS, INSTRUCTIONS AND GENERAL INFORMATION
FOR
DRIVERS, CONDUCTORS AND ONE-MAN OPERATORS

e) <u>YOUR APPEARANCE</u>

Remember these rules concerning appearance on duty:-

The wearing of collarless shirts or vests is not allowed. Shirt, collar and tie is the standard dress. Ties may be discarded during the summer months if a shirt with collar attached is worn.

Don't wear multi-coloured or gaudy shirts.

You are issued with blue shirts. Wear these or white shirts.

An unbuttoned tunic will spoil an otherwise smart appearance Get the habit of fastening the buttons.

Wear black footwear. Beach sandals and similar footwear must not be worn.

Trinkets or badges which are not part of the official uniform must not be worn.

Don't forget - Look smart - Look clean.

f) <u>UNIFORM AND EQUIPMENT</u>

The Department provides you with a uniform which must be worn when on duty. Civilian clothing must not be worn on duty or to and from duty. After six months service you will be issued with a second uniform, thereafter new uniform will be issued annually.

You must not make alterations to the uniform yourself, if it does not fit properly, return it to the clothing store.

You must make yourself available when the uniform manufacturer's representative is measuring staff for the next issue.

All staff are issued with a timetable book and a fare book which must be carried at all times when on duty.

Conductors are issued with a leather cash bag; waybill cover; ticket cancellor; strap; carrying plate and combination lock. In addition a ticket box containing a setright ticket machine is issued each day. The ticket box and its contents must be returned when going off duty but all other items of equipment and uniform will be returned only when leaving or on uniform exchange.

You will be liable for the value of any uniform or equipment lost or not returned and for the cost of repairing any damage to same (fair wear and tear excepted) and such value or cost will be deducted from your wages.

I was booked to work the week with the 'Artful Dodger' and he had improved. He didn't cut out any of the route and he even went down The Broadway later in the week! I found out why later.

He had received a brown envelope from the Traffic Office, informing him of a complaint and wanting to know why he was not operating via The Broadway, as per his running sheet? He wrote down 'forgot' and returned the sheet to the Office.

Another brown envelope reached him a week later, confirming the stopping of his merit money and that was why, when we were allocated an older bus for the second part of a spreadover duty, his eyes lit up. Drivers, as a rule, did not like older buses, as many did not have power-assisted steering, which made them hard work cornering. However, the reason for his eyes lighting-up, was the fact that the bus had been in service all morning, then parked up in Avenue Road and being an older bus, had a 'non-collected fares box' at the front of the vehicle.

Driving round the corner, he stopped the bus saying, "This is where I get my merit bonus back" and from his bag, he took a long piece of strong wire and a screwdriver. Fishing down inside the box, he ended up after about five minutes, with over two pounds in coins.

"Oi! That's the company's money you're taking!", I said.

"Yeah! So what? They take my money – I'm just getting even."

"But, that's dishonest."

"Look son. If I don't take it, someone else will. The nightshift help themselves when the bus is parked overnight."

"How do *you* know?"

"I've heard rumours, anyway, we're due away in five minutes. If you want half, say no more, son – you know what I mean."

"My conscience wouldn't let me touch that money."

"Well, I ain't got no conscience. It's me or them. You ain't going to report this, are you?"

"I've a good mind to – that's stealing!"

With that, he put the money back in the box. There was an awkward silence and we drove off. I tried to make a joke of it, saying, "Look, if you read the front of the box, it says, 'Uncollected Fares', *not* 'Staff Box'". He said nothing, just stared at the road ahead and I knew then that we had just lost that fun and the team spirit which develops between a crew working together.

I would not have reported him. It was an unwritten rule that busmen did not grass on their mates. Mainly, we were a family with a lot of friendly banter and if anybody had informed on their mates, life would not be the same in the canteen. The only kind of informing busmen did, was on passengers, who to some, it seems, were the enemy.

Dodger did lose face on our last day together. It was a Friday and he wanted to finish as early as possible, to go out drinking with his mates. We were working the Number 20 route, Bournemouth Square-Somerford. Reaching Iford roundabout, I said to Dodger, "Bus's empty".

"Is that so! This is where you get an early night, my son. Don't say Dodger doesn't look after his mates."

"And 'imself'", I said.

"Always carry one of these", he said, producing a screwdriver from his bag. "I'll show you how to fix a bus."

"But, we have mechanics to fix buses."

"Yeah, after we've fixed them." He got out and unscrewed the cover of the traffic indicator lights, took out the bulb and replaced the cover. Getting back into the cab, he said, "Oh dear! Me poor little indicators don't work. Have to tell the Inspectors".

Just at that moment, an 'intending passenger' (as they are called in company memos) walked up. "Do you go to Christchurch?"

"Nar! Ere get those front screens blanked off."

"But, you have Christchurch on the front."

"We've got India on the tyres, but we don't go there! Be another bus along in a minute."

I cleared by screens to read 'Not on Service', while Dodger got on the radio to the Inspectors in Bournemouth Square.

"Bus 236 to control – Over."

"Come in 236."

"Me indicators 'ave gone".

"Gone where?"

"When I turn them on, nuffin 'appens."

"Alright, I'll arrange a bus change. Where are you?"

"Iford roundabout. Tell you what, to save you changing it, I'll take it back to the Depot, it's only five minutes down Castle Lane."

"Ave you any passengers on board?"

"No, I might as well take it back to Mallard Road and leave it there. I'll be too late to get another bus to finish me shift, we sign off after this trip."

There was a pause and he looked at me and winked, "I told you I'd get you an early night, son. I know all the tricks, son. Show them Inspectors a thing or two!". (He called me son, although I was older than him.)

The radio broke into life, this time it was a much firmer voice. "236. Proceed back to Bournemouth Square and report *with your bus* outside the Inspectors' hut".

Dodger became agitated, "'Ang on a minute. It will take me 15 minutes to get back to the Square, I'm only five minutes from the Depot and I'm finishing soon."

"You have time on your duty to bring the bus back to the Square and let *me* have a look at it – OUT!"

Dodger was angry, "Wat a plonker!". He broke several land speed records trying to get back to the Square, but with rush hour traffic, he hadn't a chance.

All the way back, he was complaining about the Inspectors, "I bet it's that plonker Walt Pritchard in the office. He's a twit! If Dave'd been on, 'e'd 'ave said take it back to the Depot. What he wants it back it in the Square for, I dunno?".

The Inspector he was referring to, was good at his job and knew when someone was trying to pull a fast one, having worked his way up to Inspector. I can still picture him. He looked like Sergeant Bilko, with his horn-rimmed glasses. He always had a severe expression on his face and was someone you would definitely not play poker with.

One day, he got on my bus, his severe expression very evident and he said, "I've had a serious complaint about your behaviour". He paused, to give the statement effect. My mind raced to what it could be? I tried to keep out of trouble, but my humorous antics with the passengers sometimes caused letters to the Office.

Inspector Pritchard was still looking at me with a steady gaze and thinking another one of my jokes had misfired, I said, "What have I done wrong now?".

"Singing on the early morning bus, stopping the passengers from going asleep". With that and seeing the expression of relief on my face, he burst out laughing.

"Well, I enjoy the job and I sing because I'm happy at work."

"Yes, I have heard. I keep getting phone calls, saying, "One of your conductors has escaped from the mental hospital"."

"Walt, there are some miserable devils on here to work with."

"I know. Keep up the good work, Tommy."

Returning to the Artful Dodger, when we reached the Square, Inspector Pritchard came straight out of the Office with a box of spare bulbs. "Which side's not working?"

"That one," pointing.

"Got a screwdriver?"

"Er, no", stammered Dodger.

"Well, I have. There's no bulb in here. What happened to it?"

"I only drives the bus, I don't inspect it!"

By this time, Walt Pritchard was looking in the box . "No good. I haven't got a bulb that fits. Park the bus in Avenue Road and both of you catch a bus back to the Depot."

"Can't I take the bus back to the depot? I'll be finishing me duty soon."

"You can't drive a defective bus. If you're late finishing your duty, put in an overtime sheet. I also want to check the radio on this bus – it's not working properly."

"What d'yu mean? I got in touch with you, didn't I?"

Walt looked at him with a straight face and said, "The transmitting button stays on all the time. When you were talking to your conductor, I heard every word you were saying!".

Yes, Walt was someone you would definitely not play poker with.

TOMMY'S TICKLERS!

"Conductor. Do you stop at the Royal Bath?"
"What, on my wages, luv. You must be joking!"

Man waiting for bus, which pulls into the bus stop so fast, his wig blows off!
Conductor shouts, "Room for one on top!".

Conductor shouts, "Terminus!".
"Is this as far as you go", calls out a passenger.

"All change, please", shouts the driver.
Lady turns to fellow passenger, "If he thinks I'm taking my clothes off, he's got another think coming!".

ALL CHANGE

Summer always brought a large influx of foreign students into Bournemouth to learn English at the language schools, of which there are quite a large number in the town. Travelling by bus, they quickly learned two things: how to say 'please' and 'thank you' and how to count their change. More than one student thought our English currency strange, when after tendering a £20 note for a 20p fare, he found his change – in piles of pennies, of course – worked out less than £19.80p!

Most of the new students had no idea of the exchange rate, many giving a £5 or £10 note for a small fare. However, many conductors would welcome this, because now they could cash up on the move ie give away most of their change and a student would be seen sitting in their seats with piles of change.

One crew I knew, used to wait until this happened, the conductor then tipping off the driver, who would swerve the bus from side to side. This would cause piles of loose cash to fall off the seats and roll around all over the floor, to be picked up later, of course, by the crew at the end of the journey. The ordinary passengers would be surprised to find that a normally nice smooth journey, could develop into a dodgem ride!

Sometimes, when a group of students boarded, it would take most of the journey to collect their fares. There were so many notes to be changed, you would run out of loose change and most of the other passengers' loose change from pockets and handbags, which you had been forced to scrounge. By the time you'd finished collecting the students' fares, the bus would be at the end of the route. In the meantime, many passengers had got off without paying, especially if you were upstairs and most students liked to travel upstairs, as for them it was a novel experience.

However, a lot of honest passengers would hand their fare to the driver, who sometimes was dishonest and who would either keep the fare, or split it with the conductor at the end of the journey. Other drivers, when handing over the money, insisted on seeing the conductor ring off the correct tickets - they were the sort who in later years would become Inspectors!

Sometimes, the foreign students would wind up the conductor, especially those who had visited England before and who could count their change. They would make sure that they were given the correct change and also watch while the conductor issued their fellow students with their change.

After deliberately short-changing one student on a crowded bus, a conductor was embarrassed when the student said, in perfect English and a loud voice, "Do you cheat all of your foreign visitors?".

"Wat yer mean?"

"You have not given me my correct change."

"Yes I 'ave. You want to learn to count."

"I have learned to count, *after working in a international currency exchange office!*"

Other wind ups, were for groups of students to get on with £20 notes each and everyone pay his own fare. Alternatively, they would get on with piles of loose change, pay their fares and watch the conductor's cash-bag grow heavier by the minute. They would laugh between themselves, as the conductor began to walk one-sided after being given several large amounts of small change.

One day, I was walking one-sided, just as I have described above, after being given several large sums of small change, when three students got on wearing just tee-shirts and shorts. Laughing, the leader of the group offered me a £50 note for a 20p fare, grinning all over his face.

"Have you anything smaller?"

"No, sorry."

"Have any of your friends got anything smaller?" (more laughter between them).

"No, sorry."

"Are you all going to the same place?"

"Yes. We are all friends and we are all sorry to travel on your English bus with large English money."

"Sorry," said another of the group, grinning all over his face.

"You will be", I said. Then in a loud voice, to ensure that the other passengers could hear that I was not short-changing them, "Three 20p fares totals 60 pence. You have £49 40p to come in change. Hold out your hand". Then, I started counting, pennies first.

The leader, hand held out, looked on in horror, as the pennies began to fall. "No! No! No!", he cried out, "*I want notes*".

"Sorry, I've only got a £50 note", I replied.

By the time I'd finished counting out the change, all three got off with the pockets in their tee-shirts bulging and with their shorts hanging down over their ankles. As they stepped off the bus, they turned and looked at me and just before the bus drove off, I burst out laughing and said in a loud voice, *"Sorry!"*.

Another trick used by some conductors when students presented a £20 note, was to count out the change very slowly. By the time all the piles of coins had been counted out, the bus had usually passed the stop that the student had wanted to alight and many a time a conversation between the student and the conductor went like this:

"Please, could you hurry up with my change? I get off next stop."

"Hang on a minute Abdul, I'm trying to find some pound-notes in my pocket."

"No. Please – I get off!"

"Not until I've given you your change."

"No! *Please!*"

"Y'are! I think I've found some pound-notes for you."

"Please! Please! I have passed my stop."

"No, sorry I thought I had some."

"Please hurry – we are well past my stop now."

"No. I haven't got any pound notes. You'll have to have small change."

"Please! I will now have to get bus back to my stop."

"At least you'll have the right change for the conductor!"

During such interchanges, sometimes students would just flee, leaving their change with the conductor. Also, during the time taken dealing with a student, several other passengers could have left without paying, a fact totally ignored by the conductor, as getting even was more important. The students gave me many a good laugh, although sometimes they didn't appreciate the funny side – but, I always did.

One day, I was going around the top deck of the bus collecting fares, when a student handed me a piece of paper, with an address written on it. "Excuse me, Sir. Do you go there?". I looked at the address, but it didn't ring any bells.

"'Ang on a minute, I'll ask my driver – he'll know."

I went downstairs, handed my driver the piece of paper and said, "Do we go there?".

"No, but if he gets off at Tuckton Bridge, he can walk through."

Just then, the student came down the stairs and made to get off. "No, don't get off the bus just yet, I will tell you where to get off."

"No! Please, I get off."

"No! Stay on the bus until *we* tell you to get off," shouted my driver.

"No! Please, I must get off."

With that, the driver stopped the bus. Without opening the doors, he got out of his seat and began walking, up and down the full length of the lower saloon. At the same time and speaking very slowly and deliberately, he said," Walk very long, if you get off here". He then quickened his pace, to walk very fast, saying,

"Very short walk, if you get off later, *when we tell you to get off the bus*".

The other passengers just sat in their seats, mouths open, totally amazed, watching my driver taking long, then short strides up and down the bus.

"No! *Please*. Open the doors and let me get off your bus. I will be late home to my host family."

"Too right mate, if you walk from here", said the driver.

"Let him off", shouted some of the passengers, "We want to get home".

"Alright", said my mate, opening the doors, "And here's your bit of paper".

The student got off, glared at us both and walked slowly away. "Can't help some people", my driver said, shrugging his shoulders.

As we roared off, I went back upstairs to finish collecting the fares. Reaching the top deck, one of the passengers called out, "Excuse me. Have you my piece of paper with the address of the host family I am going to?".

I shot back downstairs like a bullet from a gun. "You know that student I asked you about with an address on a piece of paper?", I said to the driver.

"Yes. He got off back there."

"No, he didn't! He's still upstairs. *We've given the piece of paper with the address on it to the student who got off!*"

"Nip back up and ask him if he's got a good memory. That's the trouble with the Chinese, they all look the same. God knows how the police get on with identity parades in China?"

On another occasion, I was working a circular route from Bournemouth Square, out to Bear Cross and then back to the Square, which took about an hour to complete. A student got on and asked, "Do you go to Cemetery Junction?".

"Yes, nine pence, please."

"I am a stranger to your country, I do not know where I have to get off. Will you tell me, please?"

"Of course", I said and he took his ticket and went upstairs.

My mate called out, "You know we go the long way round to the Cemetery? We stop there on the way back from Bear Cross" (I should explain, if we had been doing the route the other way round, we would have gone to Cemetery Junction first, being only about a mile up the road).

"Oh! That's alright, he won't know that, being a stranger to Bournemouth."

It was a busy trip, although by the time we arrived back at the Square, the bus was empty. It was not often that you did the same route twice, but on this occasion that was the case and still having ten minutes till the start of our next trip, we made a quick cup of tea.

Half-way through our tea break, we saw a pair of feet coming down the stairs, followed by rest of the body of the student who had asked for Cemetery Junction. "Excuse please, are we at Cemetery Junction yet?" (we had passed it on our way back from Bear Cross and were just about to do the same route again!).

Anyway, I said, "Not yet. I'll tell you when to get off".

"Thank you" and the feet disappeared upstairs again.

My mate looked at me, "You'd better make sure you tell him next time, Tommy, otherwise he'll be giddy!".

This time around, I remembered to shout, "Cemetery Junction". With that, he came down the stairs and as he got off, he turned round and looked at me, saying, *"It's a long ride for ninepence!"*.

It was very good value. If he had gone the other way round, it would only have been 10 minutes, unless I forgot, of course, to shout 'Cemetery Junction'!

Mind you, he was luckier than another student who had sat upstairs on a bus late one night. The bus had gone back to the Depot with him still on board and the crew having forgotten to check the bus, he sat upstairs for over two hours! He had to wait until a night cleaner found him!

Although we had some fun with the students in the summer, not all the passengers found them so amusing, such as when early morning buses, full of students would go past the bus stops where people were waiting to go to work. At other times and until the language schools instructed their students in the British tradition of queuing, when they were in a queue, as the bus pulled up, many a time all the students would dash to the front to get on first, much to the annoyance of the regular passengers.

The language schools also got together with the Bus Company to make arrangements for students to buy a bus pass for a given period of time. These were very welcome to the conductors, as they did not have to collect a fare and many a conductor went to bed dreaming of having a full bus full of students, all with passes, getting on in the Square and all getting off together at the end of the route.

Others had nightmares over the loss of earnings from giving incorrect change, when offered £20 notes!

TOMMY'S TICKLERS!

After 35 years a conductor, a member of staff was made to become a one-man operated bus driver. During his first journey, the office got a call from the police informing them the bus had crashed into a shop. An Inspector drove down to the shop and asked the driver what had happened?
"Dunno," said the driver. "I was upstairs collecting the fares at the time."

A woman driver operating a one-person bus, watches a young mum with eight children struggle on board with all her shopping. "Anything I can do to help?", she asks.
"Yes. Run off with my husband!"

"How do I get to Sandbanks, Driver?"
"Take a Number 12 bus, Sir."
"But, the Number 12 does not run on Sundays."
"In that case Sir, take a Number 6."
"But, the Number 6 only goes half-way."
"Well, take two, then!"

SHUT THAT DOOR

Because sometimes conductors, for a variety of reasons, didn't come into work, there were what we called 'Rush' conductors. They were there to cover anybody who failed to turn up for duty and the job was popular, because there were no late turns. The title 'Rush' was a bit of a misnomer – they never rushed anywhere, except going home.

Anyway, one day, when signing on for duty at Mallard Road Depot, as Inspector 'Bill the Pipe' handed me the black box containing my 'setright' ticket machine, he said to a couple of the 'Rush' conductors, "'Ere, guess who 'e's got as 'is driver? *'E's got the Strouden Strangler!*".

There was roars of laughter from the rush conductors and one of them said, "Gor blimey! What a pair!".

By this time, Bill was wheezing, coughing, spluttering, all at the same time, and still with his pipe in his mouth. "I reckon this is where I gets rid of Tommy Steele once and fer all! Tommy will be singing round the bus and Strangler will put 'is 'ands rahnd Tommy's neck and all me problems will be solved."

"Never mind, Bill, I'll be thinking of you and I'll sing 'Goodbye My Love'".

"Git 'im out of 'ere! Oh God, me pore 'ead."

During my service with Yellow Buses, I came across drivers, conductors and Inspectors who had all been given nicknames relating to particular incidents they had been involved in. The 'Strouden Strangler' had been so named, because after working a late duty, he got into an argument with his conductor. Strangler, after failing to make his point, put his hands round his conductor's neck and was only stopped from strangling him after passengers managed to part them.

After a Traffic Office enquiry, Strangler was allowed to continue driving (I told you earlier in this book, that you could get away with murder, such was the shortage of drivers). It was after this incident, that the driver, who lived in Strouden Park, acquired the nickname 'Strouden Strangler'. A further twist in this story occurred a few weeks later, when the Traffic Office booked them to work together on the same duty!

My first impressions of Strangler were not good. He never smiled, had piggy eyes and he had a brooding expression the whole time. You dare not laugh or joke with him, and, of course, I had to watch my singing.

Before we started our first journey together, he said, "Remember one thing conducting *my* bus", (I was about to ask how come was it *his* bus, when I remembered he was the *Strangler!*)". "When the doors are shut, they *stay* shut. Got it, right?". I nodded. His remarks regarding the doors, I should explain. When the conductor rang the bell, the driver controlled the doors, shutting and opening them to allow passengers to alight, or board the bus and this saved the conductor a lot of time.

Sometimes, after the driver had closed the doors, a conductor would spot somebody running to catch the bus. The normal practice was for the conductor to shout, "Runner!" and the driver would open the doors again, to let the wheezing passenger in. *But, not Strangler!*

I should mention, a bus pulling away without letting a runner on, frequently was the source of bad feeling from passengers already on the bus towards the crew and you could almost feel the atmosphere of hostility. Some would even remark, after watching someone complete a four-minute-mile to try and catch the bus, "You could have waited for that old lady!".

One driver I worked with used to make me laugh, conducting a conversation with himself! He would be pulling away from the stop, spot a runner, stop the bus and the runner would get on and gasp, "Thank you, driver".

However, woe betide anybody who got on without saying 'thank you' and sat downstairs (or even upstairs). The driver would raise his voice, so that the whole bus could hear and say aloud to himself: "Thank you for waiting for me, driver, I would have been late for work, if you hadn't waited. Oh! That's alright, madam, I look after my passengers".

The runner, collapsed on the seat, gasping for breath, would be forced to mumble, "Thank you",

When they got off, he would have another go, saying to them, "Next time, say thank you when a driver waits for you".

"I would have if I had any breath left!", would come back the reply.

Strangler's insistence that when the doors were shut, they stayed shut, nearly caused an accident one day. Most drivers waited until the passengers boarding had cleared the platform, so that they could see clearly, before shutting the doors, but for safety reasons, if a bus was a bit late, some drivers would close them quickly.

We were a bit late and after boarding passengers at the Lansdowne, Strangler closed the doors with passengers still standing in front of him. As he started to pull away, a lady at the back of the platform, who was last boarding, said, "Open the door, driver". Strangler said nothing, but continued to pull away, albeit slowly, because of the volume of traffic.

"Please, open the door, quick."

Strangler spoke, "Once the doors are shut, *they stay shut.*"

By this time the bus was gathering speed and the woman screamed at the top of her voice, "*Open the door*!".

Strangler was unmoved and repeated in a tape-recorder-like voice, "Once the doors are shut, they stay shut".

Luckily, I was near the front of the bus and grabbed the red emergency handle, which opened the doors. "*Stop*!", I shouted (and I've got a loud voice). Strangler startled, stopped the bus and onto the platform, jumped a poodle, panting, still attached to the lead which the lady was holding inside the bus! Even with the low speeds we had been doing, the poor dog should have gone into the Guinness Book of records for being the fastest poodle in Bournemouth. I worked with Strangler for the rest of the week, but he never forgave me for opening *his* doors!

Another driver who received a nickname was 'The Shoeshine Boy'. One day, when he was working with me, we stopped to pick up passengers and just across from the bus stop was a shoe shop with a large notice saying 'Sale Now On' in the window. To my amazement, my mate got out of the cab, calling back over his shoulder, "I'm just going to have a look in the window". After a few minutes studying what was on offer and without another word to me, he disappeared inside the shop. The bus was still ticking over, with an almost full load of passengers sitting around waiting to continue their journey, when round the corner comes 'Sneakey Pete', one of the Inspectors.

"Where's your mate?"

Trying to gain some time, hoping he'd walk away, I said casually, "Upstairs".

"That's a funny position to drive a double-decker bus from?", said Pete, as he got on and went upstairs. Reaching the top deck, he said loudly, "He's not here".

"Er, I think he's gone to the toilet."

"Not upstairs, I 'ope?", said Pete. By this time, the Inspector was suspicious - he knew something was going on: he got off the bus; walked across the pavement; looked in the shoe shop window; then in the door and then went inside. After about three minutes, he emerged, accompanied by my mate who was hurriedly stuffing a pair of size nines into a cardboard box.

As my mate speedily climbed back into his cab, I said in a loud voice (hoping he would catch on), "Did you find a toilet in the shoe shop?".

"Yes, I found an Inspector!"

Sneakey Pete said, "I'm booking you for delaying the service" and a week later, my mate moaned to me the he had lost more merit bonus than he'd saved on the sale price of the shoes!

BOURNEMOUTH TRANSPORT

H A N D B O O K

OF

REGULATIONS, INSTRUCTIONS AND GENERAL INFORMATION

FOR

DRIVERS, CONDUCTORS AND ONE-MAN OPERATORS

g) **POINTS TO REMEMBER**

Be civil - it means such a lot and costs nothing. Try to be helpful and obliging in your manner.

Give special attention to the blind, the infirm, the aged and all others who can benefit by your assistance. Always be prepared to give a helping hand.

Avoid arguments. Try to ignore provocation and don't be sarcastic.

Remember we carry thousands of holidaymakers every year, if you do a good job, you can help to create a good impression for the department all over the country.

If passengers complain about a service, suggest politely that they should write to the department, or take their name and address and send details yourself.

If a passenger wants to complain about you do not give them further cause for complaint by becoming offensive or by starting an argument.

Let them have your badge number. If you consider it necessary put in your own report, and if you have them give witnesses names and addresses.

Help passengers on and off the bus. Close the windows if the bus is draughty and open them if the bus is stuffy.

Always try to help people if they are asking for information; the public will appreciate it a lot more if you show some interest in their enquiries but do not do this to the detriment of the collection of your fares.

If a passenger starts to ask a lot of questions and you still have a number of fares to collect, just say 'excuse me, but I have a number of fares to collect and I will come back to you afterwards'.

Call out your stopping places in a voice sufficiently loud for passengers to hear upstairs as well as downstairs. This is more important at night than it is during the day because in the darkness many passengers do not know the exact position of the bus.

Try and remember to stop at any point asked for by a passenger. This is rather difficult, especially if a number of passengers ask you to stop at various points but you can do it if you concentrate. If you should forget, then apologise to the passenger and be nice about it even if the passenger grumbles. He or she possibly does not appreciate your difficulties, but it does not make it any better by being discourteous.

Of course, it didn't help that I was walking around the bus, singing 'Shoe Shine Boy' and when the tale was related in the canteen, he quickly earned the nickname 'Shoe Shine Boy'. It was even worse when I used to sing 'These Shoes Are Made for Walking' - my mate going absolutely spare!

Another driver I worked with was called the 'Space Invader Kid'. He loved playing the electronic machines and every spare moment was spent playing them and chatting up the women (not both at the same time, of course). He, like my other mate with the shoes, had nipped off the bus, leaving it ticking over and with passengers on board. He too, was discovered by a suspicious Inspector, playing a Space Invader machine at the back of a shop by a bus stop.

The 'Space Invader Kid' had a cheeky smile and a way with women. He worked with a lady conductor (or clippie), who had never driven a bus, but who had always wanted to. He offered to let her have a ride on the front seat, if she would let him have a ride on the back seat.

One day, after returning to Mallard Road Depot with an empty bus, she got into the driving seat and she was on her second circuit of the Depot driving the bus, when an Inspector appeared and spoilt the fun. My mate was lucky, as he could have been given the sack for allowing the clippie to take the wheel, but as the bus was on private property and without passengers on board, he kept his job. However, it was never disclosed whether the clippie kept her part of the deal?

During my time as a conductor, I worked with all sorts of drivers and depending on your mate, you could have a good week, or one that was not so enjoyable. Most busmen are moaners: it's either the job that is going downhill (and uphill, as I used to joke to the passengers), the shifts, or the Inspectors, so when you got a good mate, you enjoyed your duty.

One good mate I worked with, was John Bland, who through his wisdom, taught me a lot about the job and by sheer common sense laid the foundations for me to enjoy my job (most of the time). Chatting with John in the canteen, he had been a Union representative in the past, he predicted (correctly, as it turned out), that the job would go downhill when they got rid of conductors and made it all one-man-operated (OMO) buses. (In those days, there were very few lady bus drivers - unlike today – and I suppose to be politically correct, we should really say one-*person* operated buses.)

At the time of my conversation with John, the operation was already going one-man-operated, albeit a bit at a time and in order for the Union to accept one-man buses, the Company was offering a one-man bonus, paid every six months to all drivers and conductors. The first services to go OMO were those that used the side roads, Routes 3, 6, 9, 10 etc (which were not as busy as the ones that used the main roads) ie Routes 20, 21, 22, 23 and piece by piece, the Union and the crews voted to go over to one-man-operation.

At the time, John had forecast that stress would creep into the job and he was right. As running times were cut down, we lost the five-minute tea breaks at the end of a route, which could keep you going during a busy and stressful trip on main roads. All for a bit of extra pay and a bonus! John was proved right in more ways than one. A way of life disappeared.

I'll always remember John. He was a good, old-fashioned busman, who did the job as it should be done. He taught me a lot about bus work and life. The last time I saw him was in the old Royal National Hospital in Bournemouth, when I visited him for a request record and a chat for my show on Hospital Radio.

TOMMY'S TICKLERS!

Headlines in the Daily Echo
PASSENGERS HIT BY CANCELLED BUSES!
Two ladies talking, "'Ere Ethel, how can you get ' it by a cancelled bus ...".

"Excuse me, Driver. Where can I pick up a bus for the hospital?"
"I wouldn't do that if I was you, Sir."
"Why not, Driver?"
"Well, the last man who tried to pick up a bus, ended up in hospital with a hernia – they weigh nine tons!"

"Do you go to Somerford, Conductor?"
"No."
"Well, you have 'Somerford' on your front blind."
"We've got India on the tyres, but we don't go there either!"

FOUR BELLS FOR FOUR SCOTSMEN

There were plenty who said that the people in the Traffic Office didn't have a sense of humour. The Office was responsible for rostering drivers and conductors to work the various duties and generally most crews worked together quite amicably. Some duties could seem longer than others, particularly when both crew disliked the passengers, although not everyone adopted this attitude.

Some busmen, when they found out who they would have to work with during the following week's duties (after studying the notice board), would try to change their turn with somebody else. The Traffic Office would not change the arrangements and it was then up to you if you wanted to change, you had to ask around your mates until you found someone amenable. Having found someone, you then had to complete a form called a 'Duty Change Sheet', which was then passed to the Traffic Office before you commenced that particular duty.

All this, of course, depended very much on who you were booked to work with. Some drivers had reputations and you would find it tough convincing someone that the driver in question, was not the miserable devil he had been made out to be. However, it didn't seem to make much difference to the driver in question, even when it happened on a frequent basis. The fact that the person booked to work with him had changed duties to work with somebody else, seeming not to register.

Being myself the life and soul of the party, laughing and shouting at six in the morning, I often discovered that the driver who I had been looking forward to working with, turned out *not* to be 'Happy Harry', but the 'Strouden Strangler'! In the canteen, when I came in with my mate the 'Strangler', I would be greeted with remarks such as, "Bet you're not singing with the Strangler!" and writing this, it seems ironic that a singing group called The Stranglers have made hit records in recent years.

If you had been rostered for a late duty on a Friday and Saturday night, you could have a job trying to exchange these. Friday night buses were sometimes trouble, late night drinkers returning home considerably worse for wear, with some passengers spending all their money on drink and then expecting to travel on the bus free.

To stop any hassle, a lot of conductors faced on a late night bus by a group of yobbos, would let them travel without paying a fare. The problem with this was that the following week, the yobbos would expect to travel free with another conductor – *but not me!*

Right from the start, I set my stall out. Anybody misbehaving, swearing, refusing to pay their fare, had to get off the bus. However, when sometimes faced with an ugly situation, it was difficult not to be scared, but I kept to my rules.

In those days, not many people carried knives, or were on drugs, so your chance of being assaulted were much less than it is today. In all my times on the buses, I was insulted, but never assaulted. Also, in those days, members of the public would come to the aid of bus crews, unlike today's situation, where people sit and watch bus crews being attacked.

My method was simple. I would ring the bell four times, which was a signal for the driver to perform an emergency stop. Of course, some drivers panicked, putting their foot hard down on the brake pedal, so hard, all the passengers would join him in the front of the bus!

On one occasion, on the top deck of the bus I was working on, a yobbo stood up to take a swing at me. I rang the bell four times; he missed and landed up face down on the floor, knocking the stuffing out of himself. I said to him, "That's the trouble with my driver. He's an ex-boxer and every time I ring the bell, he comes out fighting".

After the driver had brought the bus to halt, I would go up the stairs to the top saloon and shout out, "One (two or three, or any number) to get off, driver" and that would normally do the trick. If they did refuse to move, I would say, "OK! Well, the bus stays here until you get off" and then go downstairs and join the driver, which gave you extra protection, in case you were assaulted. Also, by going downstairs, this left the yobbos upstairs and when the bus did not move, the passengers would start shouting comments, such as, "Come on, pay up!", if they had refused to pay their fare, or "Get off! I want to get home". Faced with these kind of comments, the yobbos usually came down the stairs without too much fuss, ready for the driver to open the doors, so they could get off.

In circumstances such as these, they always had to get off, I never gave second chances. For two reasons: one, to teach them a lesson about not paying up; second, if you were firm, they would think twice about playing up again on a Friday night.

On one occasion, some yobbos, having refused to pay their fares, also refused to get off. I went upstairs (after the bus had been standing for ten minutes, with the engine ticking over) and said, "If you don't get off, I'll call the police and ask them to remove you".

"Please yourself, mate. Me and my mates will sort them out", came the reply and they stayed put.

I am, of course, going back to the days when we had policemen on call. Yellow Buses' vehicles were fitted with radios, so that you could contact Control and ask for assistance. Anyway, the police arrived (six of them!) and after I had explained the situation, they marched upstairs, with me behind. I pointed the yobbos out and requested that they be removed and with that, one of the officers said to them, "The conductor does not want you on this bus – you will have to leave".

"We're not getting off. We've got to get home."

"Are you going to leave the bus the hard way, or the easy way?"

"*No way!*", they shouted.

What followed next was, "Stand aside, conductor" and within seconds, the yobbos were propelled along the top deck, down the stairs and onto the pavement. Today, this most likely would not happen. Firstly, the yobbos would plead they came from a broken home (everything was broken!) and they needed a social worker to plead their case; secondly the police would be accused of using excessive force. Of course, in those days, justice was swift and on the spot.

Not many people are aware that if, for some reason, a bus crew does not want someone on their bus, they can either ask them to leave, or have them removed. Of course, you have to have a very good reason for doing this and all the right answers ready for when the inevitable little brown envelope arrives from the Traffic Office asking for an explanation. Unlike one conductor, who refused to let a passenger on his bus, because he had stolen his wife!

At the beginning of this chapter, I wrote about the Traffic Office and how they booked up drivers and conductors to work a duty together. If you were working a late duty, it was nice to see that you were booked with a 'hard' man on those routes where you knew trouble was likely to arise on late or last buses, giving you an extra feeling of security.

One night, working with my driver Chris on the last Number 20 of the day, a drunk got on and started abusing me. When I asked him to leave the bus, Chris got out of his cab and said, "*Get off!*". The drunk, a big man, turned, took a swing at Chris, but missed. With that, Chris, with one punch knocked him out, the drunk collapsing into Chris's open arms. We placed him onto the grass verge, still unconscious and then drove off.

Chris was, by the way, an ex-boxer and also a keen Southampton football club supporter. We would have many a friendly argument about our respective teams (I'm a Arsenal supporter, by the way!). I would always win by saying Southampton was only there to make up the League and provide a game and three points for my team. Once when Southampton lost by seven goals, I gave him a tin of the soft drink 'Seven Up'.

On the other side of the coin, I was booked to work a late duty with a driver nicknamed 'Nervous Norma'. I will explain. His name was Norman and he acquired the nickname while working a one-man-operated bus. Two young boys on a school special, started kicking a tin can up and down the top deck. Halting the bus, Norman went upstairs and said, "Stop that!", in a squeaky sort of voice, "Or I'll call the police". The boys ignored him and 'Nervous' ran downstairs and using his radio, informed the Inspectors that he had trouble on the bus.

The nearest police station was two minutes away at Winton and that day there was obviously a surplus of officers and police cars, so much so that half the Dorset police force, three police cars and *a riot van* were dispatched to the scene. A passing off-duty bus driver also joined in and that's how the story came out in the canteen. How two white-faced boys, were stopped from kicking a can, thus earning Norman, the nickname 'Nervous Norma', which he carried for the rest of his service with Yellow Buses.

I was booked to work with him on main road routes and about ten o'clock at night, we were on our way to Somerford, working the Number 20 route. We stopped at the Lansdowne and four drunken Scotsmen got on, somehow finding their way up onto the top deck. Now, let me say at this point, I have nothing against Scotsmen.

Once, when a Scotsman got off the bus, there was a sound of glass breaking. A bottle of whisky from under the Scotsman's coat, had fallen onto the pavement and smashed into pieces. The poor man then sat down on a seat by the bus stop and cried (it was enough to make me cry as well!). I sat down with him and between his sobs, he said it was his first day on holiday in Bournemouth and with his bottle of whisky now gone, he had lost his entire luggage. Of course, I did my best to comfort him, so as you can see, I really *do* like Scotsmen.

It seemed during my time on the buses, that I came across many Scotsmen, either drinking, or having been drinking. Most conductors would leave them alone and not collect their fare. Of course, word soon got around that if you had a Scot's accent and got on the bus haphazardly, you could travel free.

When 'Nervous Norma', my driver, saw the four drunken Scotsmen get on the bus, he went white. It was obvious the four were drunk, because as they went upstairs, they were singing 'Scotland the Brave' and calling us 'English Wankers!'. My mate said, "I'll drive as fast as I can to Boscombe Gardens, they'll get off there" (Boscombe Gardens was a favourite place for all kinds of the drinking fraternity to meet up).

"No, don't do that. I want time to go up and collect their fares."

'Nervous' looked at me and seemed to go even more white in the face. At the

same time, his nerves reducing his voice to a squeak, "Your joking?", he
squeaked.

Your'e

"Never been more serious in my life."

He looked at me with an expression of disbelief, "If you go up there, they'll
do you over".

"Don't see why they should travel free if they have money to spend on drinks
– other passengers have to pay."

By this time, 'Nervous' was driving the bus and breaking all land speed
records. "I'm going upstairs", I said.

'Nervous', with one last plea, turned towards me and said, "It's not worth it.
Think of your wife at home – you've got a lovely wife".

"How do you know?"

Not in a mood for jokes, he said, "Well, think of my wife. If we both get hurt,
who'll look after them? It's not worth it. The Company won't thank you for it".

"It's no good, Norman. When I started on here, I set out my rules – *not* paying,
then you *walk*."

"Well, if they won't pay, make them out an uncollected fare slip then."

The thought of trying to make out an uncollected fare slip, made me laugh. I
could just imagine asking them for their name and address! I could picture the
people in the Office looking at the slips and wondering where 'Jock of no fixed
abode' lived, so that the Inspector could go round, knocking on his door to
collect the unpaid fare.

As I mounted the first stair, 'Nervous' obviously giving up on trying to make
me change my mind, said, "If you get trouble, ring the bell four times and I'll
do an emergency stop". The significance of this remark did not register until later.

I climbed the rest of the stairs, to find four drunken Scotsmen sitting in the
back, singing and with their arms round each other. "Fares please", I croaked.

"Jimmy will pay."

"Which one of you is Jimmy?"

They looked at each other, then all round, *"Where's Jimmy?"*, they cried, "He's
no' on the bus!" and with that they all got up. "Stop the bus – quick", they said,
"Quick!", so, I gave 'Nervous' four bells.

Now, the bus was not only in the Guinness Book of Records for the land speed
record, but also for the quickest emergency stop. As the bus screeched to a halt,
they all pounded past me and I said, "Has Jimmy got all your money?".

"No! He's got all our whisky."

I came downstairs. There was no sign of 'Nervous', but going onto the
pavement, I saw him in the distance running ahead of the Scotsmen. Eventually,
towards the Lansdowne, they overtook him and he came back to the bus looking
very sheepish. "I was trying to find a telephone box to ring for help."

"Well, you passed one by the stop."
"Er, yes! But the phone wasn't working."
"Why didn't you use the radio in the bus?"
"It's not working."
"The only thing working is your legs."
"I would have got help for you, honest."
Just then, the radio on the bus came into life - "Bus 123 on 20 Route, come in please. Where are you?".
'Nervous', glad of the chance to avoid looking at me, jumped into the cab, picked up the receiver and said, "Bus 123 receiving".
"Where are you?"
"Er, coming up to Boscombe Gardens."
"Well, be careful if you have to stop there. A man's standing in the middle of the road waving a whisky bottle around."
"So, that's where Jimmy is", I said.
'Nervous', still looking sheepish, but also relieved, said, "Did you get their fares?".
"No. But I got a story for the book I'm going to write on this job when I retire!"

TOMMY'S TICKLER!

Mother and daughter waiting at the bus stop. Bus pulls up and the Conductor shouts out, "One only".
"You wouldn't separate a mother from her daughter, would you Conductor?"
"No madam. I did that twenty-five years ago and I've regretted it ever since."

IF YOU'RE MAD, IT HELPS!

Jasper Carrot, the comedian, asks the question, 'When the nutter gets on the bus, does he sit next to you?'.

What makes a person a 'nutter'? Let's say that they behave in public differently to you or I (well, you anyway!). The dictionary definition describes *nutter* as 'slang for a crazy person', but, of course, in today's politically correct society, they would be described as maladjusted. However, that's enough of the big words, in the 1980s, they were known as nutters and Jasper Carrot goes on to say, 'You can hear the nutter coming up the stairs. Please God! Don't let the nutter sit next to me. The nutter, meanwhile, is holding a corn beef tin in his hands, saying, "I've got an atom bomb here!"'.

One nutter who regularly used my bus and who always went upstairs, was not holding a corn beef tin, he had a radio, playing Radio One on full blast, two inches from his ear! Pandemonium would usually break out on the top deck, until I was forced to run up the stairs and force him to either turn the radio off, or he would be turfed off the bus. However, that was not the reason he was placed in the nutter category, it was because on some days, he would board the bus with the radio still clamped close to his ear, but *turned off*!

Passengers would give him puzzled looks, as the radio was not a light-weight model, but a full double-speaker job. He must have been strong to hold it with one hand, two hands being what was really needed. One day, a passenger asked him why he held the radio two inches away, but turned off – it was a conversation he wished he had never started!

"I've gone deaf", said the radio man.

"Is that why you are holding it so close?"

"No. I've gone deaf in both ears."

"Oh! You poor man. Excuse me for asking, but if you are deaf, why are you holding the radio up to your ears with it turned off?"

"Because I've nowhere else to put it."

Another passenger leaned over and said, "If you're deaf, how come you are in conversation with the person sitting next to you?".

"Pardon?"

"I said if you are deaf, how can you hear what the person is saying sitting next to you?"

"Pardon?" and with that, the nutter got up to get off. However, although I had been waiting to collect his fare when he got off, I was so enthralled with the entertainment, that I forgot to collect it. Perhaps, he was more cleverer than me?

Other nutters included a lady, who when I went to collect her fare, said, "We know all the secrets". Turning to the other passengers and pointing at me, she would repeat, "We know all the secrets". I had to laugh seeing all the passengers sitting in their seats wearing puzzled expressions. I would always reply with a passage from the Rule Book in mind ('Do Not Get Into Arguments With Your Passengers') and say simply, "Yes, luv" and she would then turn and look at the other passengers with a self-satisfied expression on her face. I came across her many times during my conducting days and never discovered 'the secrets'.

When she got on the bus, if a driver caught her eye, she would usually say to him, "We know all the secrets". One day, I was working with my short-tempered mate Ken and as she got on, he happened to glance in her direction (fatal mistake). "We know all the secrets, don't we driver?", she said.

"What bloody secrets are you talking about?"

"We know all the secrets", she repeated.

"What bloody secrets are you talking about, woman?"

As she went upstairs, she repeated, "We know all the secrets".

By now Ken was very upset. He got out of the cab and followed her upstairs. "What are you on about, woman? Secrets? What secrets?"

She sat down smiling and said, "We know all the secrets, driver".

By this time, I had run up the stairs to try to prevent Ken exploding with rage. Turning to me, he said, "What have you been saying to this daft woman? Is this one of your stupid japes? Is she a friend of yours?".

"It's alright Ken. Cool down. She means no offence."

I eventually managed to get Ken back into his cab, smoothed his feathers down and then went back upstairs and collected her fare. Again she repeated, "We know all the secrets".

At the end of the journey, I made the mistake while sitting down having a cup of tea with Ken, saying, "We know all the secrets".

With that, he jumped up, knocking his tea over, "*Just what secrets are you talking about?*".

"Ken, that's a secret", I replied. It took me the rest of the shift to scrape him off the ceiling and if ever I wanted to get Ken going in the canteen, I would say, "*We know all the secrets*".

Another odd customer was nicknamed 'The Bag Man' and his speciality was to get on your bus, clutching a large paper bag. After paying his fare, he would then go round the bus, picking up all the litter he could find. Many a passenger was surprised to be asked "Lift up your feet please, while I pick up all the paper on the floor" and when he had left the bus, he had done the bus cleaner's job – unpaid! Even before boarding the bus, he had usually persuaded passengers waiting at a bus stop, to shift their feet, while he cleared up all the odds and ends scattered around.

Later, when I became a Yellow Coach driver, he came on an excursion to Salisbury Races, complete with bag, of course. Having cleaned the interior of the coach, he then got off and proceeded to tidy up the litter on the Race Course itself!

Another, nicknamed 'The Admiral', used to stand at the bus stop in full naval uniform, complete with heavy gold braid. If the conductor was standing on the platform, when the bus pulled into the stop, he would say, "Are you going to pipe me aboard?". Some of the more unkind conductors replied with answers, the like of which my publisher refused to print in this book.

Jumping ahead a bit to my Yellow Coach driving days, he came on one excursion of mine to the Portsmouth Navy Days and spent the day walking round the docks being saluted by ratings and naval officers. The irony of this story is that in real life, his job was that of a toilet cleaner!

"Hey up, the moose has just got on!", said my driver, one day, after an elderly lady boarded our bus.

I said, "The moose? Why do you call her the moose?".

"You'll find out, but brace yourself, it won't be long coming."

Puzzled, I started collecting my fares, when a loud, deep baying sound, similar to a moose, I suppose, came from the lady in question. I almost jumped out of my skin and so did all the passengers, all except my driver, who had braced himself for just such an occurrence. During the journey, she gave several more moose calls and by this time I too had begun to brace myself. One day, working with Neil (the unkind and sarcastic driver), he said to her, as she got off, "Second road on the left for the zoo".

Another man, after paying his fare, used to get up and march up and down the lower saloon. On one occasion I had no alternative, but to say to him, "Do you mind sitting down, Sir".

"I can't", he replied, "I'm marching to London to have tea with the Queen".

Referring to another driver nicknamed Gay Gordon (because he was gay), my mate called from the cab "The queen's not in London, he lives in Bournemouth and he's on holiday". All this was, of course, lost on the rest of the passengers, who all had puzzled looks.

"No. My Queen lives in London and I'm having tea with her."

The driver again: "Bit late mate. It's six o'clock in the evening".

Still on his feet, the man replied, "I'm marching to London, to be there in time for tomorrow".

By this time, I'd had enough, he was getting in my way collecting the fares, so I said, "If you don't sit down, you'll be marching on the road, *not* on my bus". When he eventually got off, he set off up the road, swinging his arms like a regular soldier. As we went to pass him, my mate slowed the bus down and opened the doors. He shouted out, "Hey mate! You're marching the wrong way for London" and we both then roared with laughter, as he proceeded to walk round in circles. My mate's parting shot to me was, "Just imagine him stopping somebody in the street and asking the way to London – bet it'll be a foreign student?".

After relating this tale in the canteen, it seems we were not the only crew to have had him on board. One wag commented, "Bet he gets a job on Bournemouth Transport, with all the nutters we've got here".

"You speak for yourself", said my mate, clearly ruffled.

"He is!", I replied, "Some day I'm going to write a book about the antics of the passengers and the mates I work with".

"They'll never believe it!", said another.

There were other unbelievable characters who got onto the buses. One was a man who stood on the roundabout at the Lansdowne, directing traffic with a multi-coloured umbrella.

Another man regularly stood at a bus stop, playing a tuneless violin. If people did not contribute, he would stare at them with a fixed, intense expression, which usually did the trick. One day a lady got on and said, "That man playing the violin threatened me with his eyes".

My mate Neil said, "If that's all he used, I shouldn't worry".

The violin player usually did very well and very few of the public who contributed, realised that he owned a large house at Tuckton Bridge!

My favourite nutter was nicknamed 'Sooty', so-called because he would get on the bus with a Sooty glove puppet over his left hand. In his right hand, he had his fare and a big stick. After paying his fare, he would hold a conversation with Sooty and if Sooty did not come up with the right answers, he would whack Sooty hard with the stick (remember, inside Sooty was his left hand!). The conversation (much to the amusement of the rest of the passengers enjoying the free entertainment), usually went like this:

"Sooty! I'm not going to tell you again." *Whack!*

"Now say sorry." Silence - *Whack!*

"Say sorry." *Whack!*

"Come on, Sooty. I will keep whacking you until you say sorry."

Then in a tiny voice, he would mimic Sooty's voice "Sorry".

"Can't hear you." *Whack!*

Another tiny voice, "Sorry".

"That's better. What a way to behave on a bus, in front of all these people. Now say sorry to all these nice people."

Silence – *Whack!*

So, it would begin all over again, usually at least one passenger saying, "I can't stand this. I'm going upstairs".

"Don't go up there, Luv. It's not safe."

"What do mean, it's not safe?"

"No driver up there."

"Don't you start, I've had enough listening to him!"

"More than likely there's a Punch and Judy show going on upstairs", shouted out another passenger.

"No thanks, but on Friday nights on the last Number 6, Mr. Punch hits his wife Judy on the way home, after he's had a few drinks too many!", I said.

"This is just too much. I'm getting off this bus now and I'm going to report these goings on, after all, I'm only trying to get to work."

Remembering the comments in the canteen, I said, "They'll never believe it".

Sooty's act became so good, that one day another passenger, sitting apparently half-asleep next to him, as the man went to hit Sooty, he grabbed the hand holding the stick, shouting, "Leave him alone, you cruel devil".

Often, I walk along the beach at Swanage. Watching the Punch and Judy show taking place there, the thought crosses my mind, could it be my passenger from the Number 20 route who now regularly entertains the crowds of children who gather on the sand?

"That's the way to do it ...".

TOMMY'S TICKLERS!

Man with a glass eye waiting at the bus stop. Bus pulls in rather full. "Any seats upstairs, Driver. I want to have a smoke?"
"Dunno, Sir."
"Hang on, I'll just have a look", says the man
With that, he takes his glass eye out, flicks it up in the air, catches it and says, "You've got one at the back!".

Two drunks outside a bus depot, late at night.
"'Ere, Charlie, you used to be a bus driver. What about taking a bus, instead of walking home?"
"Hang on, I'll go and get one."
Thirty minutes later, he's outside with a double-decker.
"You took a long time, Charlie."
"I know. Had to move six single-deckers and coaches."
Why didn't you bring a single decker?"
"That's no good. I know you like to go for a smoke upstairs!"

Lady Conductor: Fella gets on and sits downstairs with a cigarette in his mouth.
"Oy! No smoking downstairs. You'll have to go upstairs."
"I'm not smoking."
"You've got a cigarette in your mouth."
"I've got shoes on, but I'm not walking."
"Do you want to get me into trouble?"
"Yes. What time do you finish?"

IT'S A DOG'S LIFE

One day, on studying the crew sheets in the Traffic Office, I found that once again, I'd been booked to work with Neil. He was the driver you will remember, who was tight-lipped, never smiling, sarcastic and who hated the job (but, still driving after twenty years). I thought at the time, that during my time on the Yellows, working with Neil had taken up a lot of my time. He did have a dry sense of humour, but this was reserved for the passengers, who he hated more than the job.

Passengers, on boarding the bus and seeing the driver sitting behind the wheel, would sometimes ask, "Are you the driver?".

"Na. A cardboard cut-out!"

Such remarks were always addressed to the passengers with a dead straight face, staring straight ahead. Yes, Neil was a real bundle of joy to work with!

Often, I would be walking round the bus collecting the fares and singing at the same time. Neil would say, "Why don't you shut up?".

"Cheer the passengers up, Neil. They're nearly as miserable as you."

"You don't want to go cheering them up. Tell you what, this job would be alright, if we didn't have to carry passengers."

On one occasion, half way through my duty, I was collecting fares at the rear of the bus on the top deck, when I heard voices raised in anger, coming from downstairs at the front of the bus. After a minute, the bus was still ticking over at the stop, so I went to investigate.

As I neared the top of the stairs, I could hear Neil shouting, "Git 'im off! Git 'im off, or I'll call the police". Reaching the bottom of the stairs, I saw a man holding a lead attached to a very large dog, both soaking wet.

"I'm *not* 'aving 'im on 'ere – 'e's soaking wet – and he's filthy!"

"Don't you call my dog filthy", said the irate intending passenger.

"*Well 'e's not getting on my bus!*"

The passenger then turned to get off the bus, remarking, "And you're supposed to be a public servant".

99

"I may be a public servant, as you calls it, but I'm not *your* servant."

In all my years of service, I found the words 'public servant' enraged busmen more than swearing at them, or calling them names and after the passenger called Neil a public servant, he stood no chance of travelling. As the passenger stepped onto the pavement, he said, "It's pouring with rain. How am I going to get home?"

"Throw a saddle on 'e's back and ride 'im!", called out Neil, pointing at the bedraggled dog.

Clearly put out, the passenger said, "I don't like your attitude one little bit. Your General Manager Mr. Cunningham, is a personal friend of mine and I'm going to report you – I've got your number".

I didn't say anything, but inwardly felt sorry for the person and his dog. After all, it was a very wet day, perhaps the bus behind would let them travel?

We were due to have a nice long tea break at Christchurch, so I decided to have a word with Neil. We sat upstairs with the doors firmly closed, but despite this, some passengers were already waiting to board. I knew from experience not to ask Neil to let them on and allow them to sit downstairs out of the rain.

After pouring our teas, I said to Neil, "Will you get into trouble if that passenger reports you to Mr. Cunningham?".

"Na!" Silence.

"Neil, what does the Rule Book say about allowing dogs on the bus?"

Neil looked into his cup, "It's at the conductor's or driver's discretion".

"What's *discretion*?"

"Don't let them on, mate."

"If a passenger gets on with a dog, should they be muzzled to stop them fighting?"

"What, the passengers? Yes mate, they should be muzzled alright."

"No Neil. If you had two dogs on the same bus, they could start fighting."

"No chance of that."

"Yes there is, if the dogs were both downstairs. Two dogs facing each other in a confined space, could snap at each other."

"No chance of that, if in the first place you don't let one dog on. I hate dogs. One got me reported once and I never even met 'im!"

"How's that?"

"I'll tell yer."

"Neil, its raining. Shouldn't we let those passengers waiting get on?"

"Bugger them. Wait until I tell you how this dog got me reported". With that a glint came into his eye. "I'm pulling into the stop, see. Open the doors for this woman to get off. It's dark. She gets off and steps onto a pile that a dogs left on the pavement". Obviously enjoying himself relating this story, he continued,

"She skids: one leg goes one way, the other the other way; she almost did the splits. I laughs. She turned round and says, 'I'm reporting you for this!'. At this point, he chuckled (the first time I had ever seen him smile) and said, "Why? I didn't do it!".

At that point, I said, "Maybe we had better let the passengers on and go?".

With that, Neil reluctantly got up and went downstairs. He adjusted his driving seat backwards and forward, until he found a position that suited him. Then he started the engine. Waiting for the engine to warm up, he took a handkerchief from his uniform coat pocket, carefully wiping the condensation off the inside of the windscreen. Then, using the same handkerchief, without a second thought, he slowly and methodically wiped his nose. With a distainful glance, he watched the clearly anxious crowd waiting at the bus stop to board, saying (with obvious relish), "Let's keep them out there just a little bit longer". You know, I'm convinced that if Neil had been allowed to use his discretion regarding letting passengers board the bus – as the Rule Book directed – he would have interpreted this by running around with a completely empty bus!

During my time conducting, dogs provided the sources of many funny stories. Take the time a large Alsatian dog ran onto the bus, while we were waiting at the stop by Kinson Green. I didn't see him, as he loped up the stairs, neither did my driver who had been intent on reading his newspaper. After collecting all the fares on the top deck, I realised nobody had paid for the Alsatian, who was sat panting at the back of the bus.

"Whose dog is this?", I asked. Blank stares from all the passengers. "Somebody hasn't paid for the dog – he has to have a ticket to travel." More blank looks.

"Perhaps, he's got a Rover ticket?", said one wag.

"He got on at Kinson – didn't see anybody get on with him", said another.

I went downstairs and told the driver. He said, "Ask the passengers downstairs, if they have a dog upstairs?".

"Excuse me, does anybody own a large dog Alsatian riding upstairs?" More blank looks.

"What do we do now?", I said to my mate.

"Hang on a bit, help's at hand, we're just about to pick up an Inspector", he said, as we pulled into the stop. He continued, "Don't tell him about the dog – see if he spots him!".

"Morning", said the Inspector, "What are you two idiots grinning at?".

"It's the way you have your hat on", said my mate, who was a well-known, witty person to work with. Fellow workers in the canteen had nicknamed him 'Stan' and me 'Bob', after the two characters who played the driver and conductor in the TV series 'On the Buses'

By this time, the Inspector had removed his hat, looked in the interior mirror and replaced the hat on his head. "I'm sorry Inspector, you haven't got the right shaped head to go with the hat, perhaps, if you had an operation, it might fit?".

"The only operation I want is for you two to get this bus moving and these people to work – come on now. I knew as soon as I saw you two idiots working together, I was going to have problems." Then, turning to me, he said, "Is the bus ready for me to check?".

"As ready as it will ever be – all present and correct."

"That'll be the day when *your* bus is present and correct."

My mate interrupted, "Excuse me, Blakey. If you found someone without a ticket on the bus, would you book them?"

The Inspector turned to my driver, "Don't call me *Blakey*. I'm fed up with being compared to that Inspector on the television. Only the other day, I checked a school special and all the kids kept calling me Blakey!" – we both laughed.

"It's nothing to laugh at, we should be treated with respect. In the old days, it took years to rise to the post of Inspector."

"Just shows you how the job's gone downhill now", said my mate.

"And *uphill*", I joked.

"Right! Let's check your bus and if I find someone without a ticket, *I'll book you!*" (term used when an Inspector finds something wrong on your bus and submits a report to the Traffic Office).

"That's right, Inspector", said my mate, "It says in the dictionary that the word *inspect* means to 'look carefully'". With that, the Inspector walked into the lower saloon, "Tickets pleez. Have your tickets ready for checking".

Meanwhile my driver had burst into song: 'How much is that doggie in the window? I do hope that doggies for sale'.

"Never mind the singing", I said, "I've got an idea".

"Well, treat it carefully – it's in a strange place!"

"Well, I'm strange anyway."

Next minute, I heard feet thudding downstairs, followed by the Inspector and the sounds of 'Whoof, Whoof, Whoof!' from the upstairs of the bus. The Inspector, looking disarrayed, his hat over his eyes, said, "Who let that ruddy dog on – *you*?", looking at me pointedly.

"No! He got on by himself without asking."

By this time, we had reached Kinson police station and I said to my driver, "Keep the doors shut, I'll go in and report it".

Inside the police station, sat a rather large policeman, who asked, "That your bus outside - got problems?".

"No. I've come in to ask you for directions on how to get to Bournemouth Square." He looked at me in total disbelief. "Only joking! I've got a passenger who won't pay his fare, or get off and I'd like you to remove him from my bus."

"Alright", he said, getting up and putting his hat on. As we walked towards the bus, the sounds of 'Whoof, Whoof, Whoof' could be heard coming from the inside of the bus. I said to the policeman, "I think I should tell you that the passenger is a rather large Alsatian dog".

The policeman looked at me carefully for a few seconds and said, "I recognize you now. You're that joker Tommy Steele who appeared in the Bournemouth *Evening Echo* the other night!".

"That's right", I said, He was referring, of course, to an article which had appeared in the *Echo* on my attempts to become a stand-up comedian and because of another well-known Tommy Steele, who had borrowed my name. Because of this, I had to change my name and that's why people sometimes still call me Tom Barry, from my stage and Hospital Radio presenting days. On stage, I used to call myself 'Barry Docks' and people used to think that with a name like this, I was Welsh, however, because my act sank so many times, I renamed myself Tom Barry, a name I liked. and used for many years.

Anyway back to the Alsatian. As soon as the policeman found out what he was expected to remove from the bus, he had gone back into the police station, returning eventually with a long piece of rope. "Blimey!", I said, "You're not going to hang him, are you?".

Reaching the bus, we were greeted with the sight of the dog sitting on the platform, having come downstairs, with the Inspector cowering behind a seat at the rear of the bus. The officer shouted, "Open the door, driver" and with one movement, he threaded the end of the rope through the animal's collar. "Come on, Jason", said the policeman and with the dog trotting quite contentedly at his side, he turned to return to the police station.

My mate said to the officer, "Oh! You know him, do you?".

"Yes, he often runs away from home."

"Unhappy is he?", cracked my driver.

The Inspector, satisfied that the dog was under control, came to the front of the bus and having regained his composure, became more official, "I'm going to have to report this. When I got on and said, 'Is the bus ready for checking', you never told me that you had a stray dog on board – you said, 'all present and correct'" and he took out his notebook

"Before you write anything in that notebook, I think we should make a deal", said my mate, "You don't book Tommy Steele and we do not tell them in the canteen how you ran away scared of a dog."

The Inspector looked at him, put his notebook away and said, "We've wasted enough time. Get this bus moving, but before you do, let me off – I've had enough of you two". I never heard another mention of this incident, but whenever that particular Inspector got on my bus, I sang, 'How much is that doggie in the window?'.

A rather sad story concerning a dog, happened when a man getting off the bus with a dog on a leash, said that he was sorry his dog had wet all over the platform. He said, very apologetically, "I'm taking him to the vets to be destroyed. You see, I have a new wife and she does not like dogs, so I'm having him put down".

Neil, my sarcastic driver, said, "I should have *her* put down, mate!".

Who says dogs do not have sixth sense - that dog knew he was going to die – it's uncanny.

A blind man used to get on the bus at Wallisdown and his dog used to lay on the floor of the bus and appear to go to sleep. One stop before Winton Banks, where the man would normally get off, the dog would wake up and stand up ready to get off. This happened several times during my conducting days and that dog never missed once.

If I say 'Mad Ketch', any former busman will know what I mean. He used to be regularly seen pushing an old pram, with a dog sitting in it and on reaching a bus stop, he would leave the pram while he got on the bus. The dog would quickly hop out of the pram when the bus came along and go up onto the upper deck. If the front seat was free, the dog would quickly make himself at home, enjoying himself looking out of the front window. 'Mad Ketch' was completely impervious to any angry remarks from conductors, particularly about the dog which was losing his hair, a lot always remaining on the seat when he got off.

During a hot summer's day, a lady got on my bus with a dog dripping sea water and covered in sand. She allowed the dog to sit on a seat, forcing me to say, "Why don't you put him on the floor, instead of that nice, clean seat?".

"Because the floor's very dirty!", she retorted.

Another time, while collecting fares, I reached out to take a lady's fare and sat on her lap was a small dog. As the lady handed me the money, the dog jumped up and down and bit my sleeve. "Sorry", she said, "I meant to tell you he does not like men in uniform".

Yes, conducting can sometimes be a dog's life!

SUPERSTAR TOMMY

Speaking to an audience of retired Post Office workers recently, I found myself introduced as 'The World's Most Famous Driver'. How did it all come about?

One day, arriving for work, I was given a letter. All that was written on the envelope, were the words "Superstar Tommy', The World's Most Famous Bus Driver, Mallard Road Depot, Bournemouth'. Anyway, thanks to the good old Post Office, the letter was safely delivered into my hands. The description 'Superstar Tommy' had accompanied a photograph of yours truly which had appeared in a national newspaper, as well a lot of other national and local media coverage, following several exploits of mine which had hit the headlines. I received lots of other letters addressed simply: 'The Singing Bus Driver, Bournemouth' and each time the Post Office came up trumps.

Going back to this period in my career on the buses, following the articles in the newspapers and on the radio, everytime I walked into the canteen, my mates would all burst out singing, 'He's a Star! He's a Star!'. For years, my ambition was to become a stand-up comedian on a cruise ship (the nearest I ever got to that was telling jokes to the crew on the Sandbanks-Studland chain-link ferry!).

I took numerous verbal hidings from drunken audiences in pubs and late night clubs and I soon learned how to handle hecklers. However, I still have the mental scars of compering a striptease show at Portsmouth – three minutes of nice, clean repertoire - with sailors making up most of the audience!

Another time, compering a strip show at Tidworth Army Camp, again with a nice, clean act. I thought the squaddies were all shouting, "Get 'em off!" (well, it sounded like it). Instead, they were shouting, "Get 'im off!". On many occasions they were still booing the act before me, all the way through my act (or so I thought!).

How these bookings came about was through my agent – a lady stripper, who took her clothes off on stage and then did a fire-eating act. My act and my comedy was so clean, I was the only one in the audience who appreciated the fire eating.

One night, I was booked to perform in front of an audience of greengrocers, who ended up throwing tomatoes at me. This wouldn't have been so bad, if only they'd taken them out of the tins first!

You may find this hard to believe, but I'm glad to have had these tough stand-up experiences. These situations taught me a lot about how to handle an audience and these days, I can handle the toughest after-dinner speaking engagement, although I never get heckled from my public speaking audiences today.

The only time I have been heckled was when I was addressing a group of about a dozen Women's Institute members, in a small village way out in the country somewhere. One of the audience, a little old lady, kept shouting out comments. I eventually managed to quieten her down by saying, "Why can't you go to sleep like the rest of the audience?".

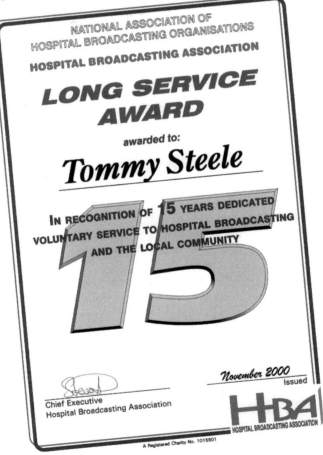

NATIONAL ASSOCIATION OF HOSPITAL BROADCASTING ORGANISATIONS

HOSPITAL BROADCASTING ASSOCIATION

LONG SERVICE AWARD

awarded to:

Tommy Steele

IN RECOGNITION OF 15 YEARS DEDICATED VOLUNTARY SERVICE TO HOSPITAL BROADCASTING AND THE LOCAL COMMUNITY

November 2000
Issued

Chief Executive
Hospital Broadcasting Association

HBA
HOSPITAL BROADCASTING ASSOCIATION

A Registered Charity No. 1015501

On this occasion, my speech, called 'It's only the passengers who run on time', caused a lot of merriment, when having gone well over the time I had been allotted for speaking, one or two members of the audience, waiting for me to finish, ended up missing their bus, resulting in me having to take them home in my car.

About this time, I joined Hospital Radio Bedside (HRB). This came about by a passenger who had listened to me joking on the bus, saying, "Why don't you come along to the studio" (then above the Eye Hospital in Westbourne) "and tell the patients a few of your jokes and cheer them up?".

"Or, get them out of hospital quicker!", said my mate who had been listening to the conversation.

I remember the first time I went 'on air' as a guest and telling some funny bus stories. After the show, I got chatting and when I said that I had over 200 comedy records in my personal collection, I was immediately invited to join Hospital Radio and become (after training) a presenter.

Two programmes not on HRB at that time, were country music and a comedy show and I suggested, as I also had a large collection of country records, that, perhaps, I could present such a programme? I was asked, "What do you know about country music?".

"Nothing", I said, "But I've a good ear for a tune and I know a man who does know a lot about country music - Bill Sykes". I would like to mention here that I worked with Bill and had many laughs with him, although these stories have been held over for inclusion in my next book. Bill taught me so much, that I was soon presenting a programme called 'Easy Country', which continued for many years and I even went as a guest on other radio stations, such as 2CR, Radio Solent and East Anglia.

My first comedy show was called 'You can laugh', which ran for many years with the title 'Laughter the best medicine'. At first, I played comedy records and told jokes and in no time at all, people were writing and ringing up asking for more. The word got around to the then BBC South 'Today' programme, who contacted me and asked if they could come down and film me for their series 'A Day at Work'. This included a session on the bus telling jokes to people to cheer them up, then back to the studio to record my show. A funny scene in the film, shows me telling jokes to a lady on the bus. Although she refused to laugh, she kept asking if she was on TV, as she wished to make a complaint about the bus service! Of course, it all made interesting viewing, although it was bit disappointing to find that out of the six hours spent filming, only about six minutes was actually used on the BBC's South Today news programme. However, I am reliably informed that some of the material not shown, kept everyone at the BBC Christmas party that year, in stitches!

On another occasion and after one of my funny stories was told on the Derek Jameson show – BBC Radio Two – I received an invitation to appear on the show. Needless to say, I spent a very enjoyable 10 minutes telling the nation about some of the funny things that can happen on a bus.

I had a lot of fun with Hospital Radio, which broadcasts to six hospitals, namely: Westbourne Eye Hospital, Poole Hospital and Poole Maternity Hospital, Wimborne, Christchurch and last, but not least, Bournemouth. Before the new broadcasting studios at the Royal Bournemouth Hospital were built, the studio was at the top of the stairs in the attic at Westbourne Eye Hospital.

One of my games at Westbourne while broadcasting my show, was to run down to the ward below, find somebody listening with earphones to my broadcast and ask them, "What do think of the show?" (I didn't tell them who I was, so I always received an honest answer).

One old man I asked, "Load of rubbish, but there's nothing else on".

"What sort of comedy do you like?", I asked.

"Don't like comedy. I like classical music."

With that, I quickly ran back upstairs to the studio, pulled a classical record out of the racks and it on the turntable. Then I switched on my microphone and as the record that was playing came to an end, I announced, "And now for the gentleman in Cornea Ward in Westbourne who does not like comedy, we have a classical record – after all, Hospital Radio is the *patients'* station". I would have dearly loved to have seen the look on his face!

The trick of ensuring that your programme was still being broadcast when you nipped downstairs, was to ensure a long-playing comedy record was on the turntable. This gave one time to run downstairs, speak to somebody, then run back up the stairs and announce the next record. The stairs were very steep and after arriving back out of breath, the listeners must have thought when I announced the record, that I had breathing problems, because I was wheezing so much (either that, or the programme had got me excited!).

Often, I would be sitting alone in the studio, doing my show and one night, I ran downstairs as usual, then back up, only to find that the studio door had slammed shut, locking me out. I knew that I had about two minutes of playing time left on the record, before the programme went silent. As the key to the door was in the studio, the only way to get back in was to run down to the bottom of the stairs, out of the front door, round the corner, up the fire escape and try and climb through the attic windows.

At the time, I was presenting my Country & Western music show, called 'Easy Country' and I always dressed for the part, presenting the show in full cowboy gear: Stetson hat, cowboy shirt, six-gun strapped around my waist and boots. Of course, you should have seen the looks on the faces of the people seeing a cowboy dash past them as I ran out of the building, round the corner and up the fire escape! In the event, the attic window proved too tight. I got jammed half in and half out and I knew that any second now, the record would stop playing and the programme fall silent.

About the same time, I saw flashing blue lights and heard the sound of heavy boots pounding up the fire escape stairs. It was dark and I had to wait until the boots came nearer to discover two policemen. They had been called to a suspected break-in by a worried resident in a property opposite. "Well, well! What 'ave we got 'ere?", said one of the policemen, looking suspiciously at my cowboy gear, "John Wayne trying to get into the Westbourne Eye Hospital".

As you can imagine, it took a lot of explaining and after a lot of heaving and tugging by the two policemen to release me from the attic window, I found myself being escorted down to the matron. She confirmed that several patients had asked what had gone wrong with their radios, as they had gone silent? With the matron's assistance in locating another key, I eventually got back into the studio and I resumed broadcasting by saying that the last twenty minutes of silence had been a sound track from a Charlie Chaplin silent film. You may be surprised to learn that one listener actually believed this!

One of my favourite comments made by a patient, was after introducing myself and my programme to him while visiting the wards collecting requests to broadcast on the show. As I was leaving, I said to him, "I hope you get better".

He replied, "And I hope your show does as well". Well, what's that saying, 'You can't please all the people all the time'!

I believe that I was put on this earth to make people laugh and cheer them up and I think I've succeeded 95% of the time. It makes me smile when I hear today's stars (who are getting paid a lot of money), say they are too tired to do many shows. I used to get up at six in the morning, work a twelve hour split shift (with overtime in the middle), dash to the studio, prepare my show, go on air, entertain the patients for sometimes two hours, get home at midnight, then get up at six next morning for another twelve hour shift. I'm sure I got more enjoyment and more laughs than the stars.

Before I end this chapter on Hospital Radio, just let me explain the funny stories I have related to you in this book. I hope I have not given the impression that Hospital Radio Bedside (HRB) is an amateur set-up – far from it. Sometimes you see on television, so-called comedy programmes where actors take the Mickey out of Hospital Radio, such as somebody running around with an old microphone talking to people in bed. Today's HRB is broadcast from two modern, well-equipped studios, located in a purpose-built building at the rear of the Royal Bournemouth Hospital, which broadcasts 'Cover Landlines' (which means the general public cannot tune into HRB) to six local hospitals.

As I have said before, HRB is the patients' station and provides the only hospital request programme for patients in local hospitals, family and friends being able to request a record for a loved one in hospital from the large selection of records held.

I cannot convey to you the feeling of joy I get from Hospital broadcasting. All members of HRB are unpaid volunteers, but not knowing this, I was sometimes asked by my mates on the buses, "How much do you get paid?". Somebody else once said, "With your show, you must be on thousands". I always answered, "In life, money and sex are the two things that people seem to want most and both are often misused".

I also enjoy very much listening to comedy records and recently, Peter Foster, a fellow volunteer on the Swanage Steam Railway, invited me to his Dorchester studio, to record some programmes for Ridgeway Radio and Talking Books for the Blind. We spent the afternoon recording four half-hour shows and had so many laughs in the process, that my sides hurt from laughing so much.

I consider myself a lucky person to have laughed all my life and what follows dear reader, is a little motto you might like to consider:

Laugh and you live longer,
The longer you live, the more you laugh.

When we think of the word 'star', it reminds us of something that twinkles in the sky and I would like to think I twinkled on radio.

There's a song, which goes something like this, 'If I can help somebody as I go on my way, then my living shall not be in vain'. Over the years, I have helped many passengers as they went on their way. I've held several certificates over the years for safe driving and millions of passengers used my bus, all arriving at their destinations safely.

I enjoyed my job, with lots of laughs every day and through working on the buses, I found Hospital Radio. Hopefully, I made people, worried and in pain, laugh and through comedy records, take them on a journey of laughter.

TOMMY PUTS THE BUSES TO BOOK

When I sat down to write this book, little did I know that I had over a thousand pieces of paper in my collection of stories, mainly humorous, but some sad, which had occurred during my years of service on the buses. Funny stories occurred all the time and when they did, I used to grab the nearest piece of paper to me in the cab (sometimes the Vehicle Report sheet!) and scribble down what had happened, so that I would not forget.

Many a time I've been driving along, spotted something funny, burst out laughing aloud and as soon as it was safe to do so, pulled the bus over and stopped by the side of the road. I would then quickly grab some paper, jot the story down and drive off. Looking in the mirror inside the cab which allowed me to look back into the interior of the bus, I would see the open-mouthed expressions of my passengers and this would start me off laughing all over again, although I frequently noticed after such incidents, people gave me a wide berth when they got off the bus.

I once cleared the bottom deck of a crowd of Chinese students, when I started singing the 'Ying Tong' song from the BBC radio programme - the Goons - the words going something like 'Ying tong, ying tong, idle I po'! For days afterwards, I wondered if there was a sinister meaning in those words – if you were Chinese? Or was it my singing? No, it couldn't be!

Mae West, the film star famous for her quotes, once said, "Keep a diary. One day it will keep you". Well, I have never been organised enough to keep a diary, but I once bought a book entitled 'How to Organise Yourself in One Day', then lost it! However, my recollections have kept people laughing at my After-Dinner speaking engagements for years now.

I'm sometimes asked, "Are you making these stories up?", or "Does all that really happen on a bus?". Dear readers, even the most comic mind could not make up some of my experiences and I know this from personal experience, as I used to be a stand-up comedian. In fact, the night comedy died, I was held for questioning! As a former comedian, I can see the funny side of life and human nature, if you study it, can be very funny.

For example, the way some people drive their cars. Can you imagine walking along the pavement behind someone walking slowly, saying 'Come on, pull over - I want to get past!'; or perhaps , a 25-stone person blocking the pavement and you're saying 'Wide loads should travel at night'. You see what I mean? My sense of humour will always see the funny side of life and I frequently say to people, "My face is my fortune". The usual reply is, "How come you're always broke then?".

I count myself very fortunate that I was born with a sense of humour, as this has kept me out of a lot of possible arguments when working on the buses and at this point, I would like to thank you – the passengers – for giving me so many laughs by your behaviour.

As I have already commented in this book, a driver once said to me, "This job would be alright, if we did not have to carry passengers". Of course it wouldn't be alright if we didn't carry passengers! There wouldn't be any fares, so there would be no wages and I would not have been able to write a book of funny stories going back to 1979, my first day in the Training School at Mallard Road Bus Depot in Bournemouth.

The first words I can remember from Inspector Dennis Buxton (later Chief Inspector and a good one at that) to myself and the other prospective bus men in my class, was "Good morning lads, welcome to Bournemouth Transport" – as it was known before being given a new coat of paint and a new image. The Inspector continued, "To the *right* person, bus work is a wonderful job, but to the *wrong* person, it's crucifixion".

So, What's a 'right' person? Well, one that's honest; conscientious; has a good temperament; is smart and has the ability to turn a deaf ear to comments made in a loud voice by a passenger boarding, such as, "Where have you been? Your *late*!". All this and having to get out of bed at 4.30 a.m. in the morning for an early shift, or turn, as they were called then.

Throughout the rush hour, struggling with a bus 8 feet 3 inches wide and 39 feet long and in case of low bridges, being aware that you vehicle was 14 feet high. Loading and unloading some 200 passengers on a journey into Bournemouth Square and that was in the days when you had conductors and there was far less traffic on the roads. Of course, nowadays, most of those passengers are sitting mainly one person per car, *in front of your bus*! When you had a conductor with you, you could usually laugh it all off, over a cup of the best tea it was possible to taste – from a vacuum flask – in a short break at your terminus. Many a cup of tea and quick smoke has saved arguments on the return journey. I have seen some drivers after a tough journey, smoking so quickly, it was like watching a condemned man facing a firing squad. Bus work in those days was fun and I often meet busmen I worked with in the 1980s, many recalling amusing funny incidents from those times.

However, spare a thought for today's one-person-operated buses and I say 'one person' deliberately, because today there are more woman bus drivers than men. With the modern operating methods, you not only have to fight the traffic and keep to the timetables, you also have to take money, issue tickets and take a lot of verbal abuse, not only from yobbos, but also from normally decent people who, perhaps, are late for work.

I sometimes think back to my sense of humour at this period, when faced with a remark from a passenger waiting for my delayed bus, such as, "Your late! I've been waiting half an hour for you" and I would reply, "You're lucky! My mother waited *nine months* for me!", a story that would be retold to other busmen in the canteen, resulting in laughter all round. This would frequently trigger off other funny stories that my mates had experienced, such as, "We left this runner (a term used for an intending passenger chasing a bus after it had left the stop without him) behind, but he was obviously some runner, because several stops further on and due to the traffic, he caught us up! Anyway, panting, he climbed on board and guess what he said?". We all waited expectantly …

"Thanks for not waiting for me. I've run a whole fare stage and saved five pence!"

Of course, everybody laughed and I said, "You should have told him to run behind a taxi".

Somebody said, "Why?".

"That way, he would have saved more money."

Well, we've spoken about the 'right' type of person to be a busman, but what about the 'wrong' type? For bus work, the one that faces crucifixion every day he works, is one that can't get out of bed on time for an early turn; is surly; does not get on with people and is quick to take offence at remarks made by passengers or colleagues.

One such person was Dan (not his real name). Dan had a reputation for having a quick temper. A lot of conductors did not want to work with him and if they were booked to work with him, they would look through the duty roster several weeks ahead to try and swap duties. They would sidle up to you in the canteen and say, "Hello, Tommy, my old mate, how would you like a nice early turn, instead of the nasty late one you are booked for in six weeks'time. It's a real pig of a turn – I worked it last week. Always get trouble with the yobbos on the last bus, when I worked it on Friday night (Friday was always a bad night. It was pay day and the yobbos would spend all their money on drink). Six yobbos upstairs, threw most of the seats out of the emergency door window".

I replied, "Thought there was no standing allowed upstairs?".

The other conductor forced himself to laugh, saying, "Sign here" and quickly handed me the Duty Change sheet to sign before I changed my mind.

Talking of Dan, one morning he had his mate pinned against the side of the bus, fist raised saying, "I'll do you if you say that again" and that was before the bus had even left the Depot!

On the first occasion I worked with him, he said, "Tommy Steele? You're that clown who's going around telling jokes and singing to the passengers – *you're an idiot*!".

"What are your qualifications on judging me to be an idiot?", I asked.

"What do you mean?", Dan replied.

"Well, some of us are only acting!"

"I dunno what you mean", said Dan looking perplexed, "But if you're trying to be funny, watch it".

I said, "My old mum used to say to me, don't go on the stage telling jokes Tommy – people will only laugh at you. She was wrong. I tried to be funny on the stage for years as a comic, but never made it".

"Yeah! I've heard some of your jokes and they definitely aren't funny."

"It's no good being serious, Dan – you will never get out of this world alive!"

"Nor will you, if you don't shut up. I want no jokes or singing while you're with me. *Alright*?", his hackles starting to rise. After having worked one day with Dan, I found a new conductor who jumped at the chance of changing his nasty late turn for a nice early turn, although unknown to him, with a nasty driver.

One story concerning Dan that went around the canteen, raised a few laughs, was when he changed his driving duty for a conducting duty (if you were a driver, you could change duties with a conductor, providing the conductor had passed his bus driving test and had a licence to drive). You can imagine the funny results of a conductor trying to drive a bus, who hadn't passed his test (mind you, some of the drivers I worked with, drove like that anyway!).

I should explain, conductors having recently passed the test to drive a bus, were known as 'wheel happy'. They enjoyed (well, some anyway) driving a bus, as long as the vehicle was fitted with power-assisted steering – we still had a few older buses in service without it. I'll explain. Power-assisted steering makes it easier for the driver to turn the steering wheel, because it's lighter and when you are in and out of traffic all day, this makes a big difference. I have even seen some buses carrying a full load of passengers, with the driver having to stand up to pull hard on the wheel to steer the bus round a corner.

I mentioned earlier 'Vehicle Report sheets'. These were kept in the cabs of the buses, so that the driver could write down any faults found on the bus. When the bus returned to the Depot, the sheets were handed in and the Depot mechanics would duly make any repairs required. If these proved to be minor and it was Summer service with a consequent shortage of buses, after a cursory inspection, the vehicle frequently went back into service with the fault unrepaired.

In the Winter, it was always windscreen demisters that didn't work and you would found yourself driving a bus with the impression that you were sitting in a chip shop, instead of warm air blowing on the windscreen! Despite giving the screen a quick wipe with your hand, the mist would quickly return and particularly at night and when it was raining, sometimes you had to guess where you were going. Such faults should, of course, have been fixed in the summer and the winter always appeared to come as a surprise to the garage staff. One day, my bus was so cold, two eskimos got off and complained it was too cold to travel in!

Back to power-assisted steering. One driver who submitted a bus Vehicle Report sheet, wrote, 'This bus's steering is so heavy, it's easier to drag a rapist off my sister, than drag this bus round a corner!'. As to be expected, he was called into the Traffic Office for making 'facetious' remarks, but as he didn't understand what the word facetious meant, they let him him off!

Anyway, back to Dan's story: Having found a 'wheel happy' new driver, Dan changed with him and did the conducting. Everything was fine, until a passenger offered his fare and said, "Twenty-five pence, Hogshead". *It was like putting a match to a can of petrol!*

"Don't you call me Hogshead – *Fishface!*", shouted Dan.

"I'm not. I want to go to the Hogshead pub in Westbourne", said the shaken passenger.

Dan did not change his duty again after that, but kept to driving, where he didn't have to meet the public and when they got on and said, "Good Morning" to him, he could look out of the window and ignore them.

One day and off duty, he got on my bus with his wife. He introduced me as "That idiot, Tommy Steele. You know, Luv, that one I was telling you about. The one that sez to the passengers getting on the bus, 'break into a walk; don't forget to wipe your feet, I've just hoovered the bus; tea room upstairs', that sort of thing"! The funny thing was that he was laughing, something I'd never seen him do at work.

At a later date, I said to him, "I've never seen you laugh at work".

His reply was, "It's the job innit. *I hate it* and I hate the public – they always get you into trouble, reporting you". Dan, I should say, retired at sixty-five years of age, after many years of hating the job. I still see him around on occasions and a more happy person you could not wish to meet. In fact, he told me he was looking forward very much to reading my book.

I always enjoyed the job. No two days were the same and in this, my first book,

I'm going back to the fun days of bus work. Buses operated by a driver and conductor, were rapidly disappearing as one-man-operated buses began to make inroads, with the result that today's bus drivers do not have the same opportunities to learn the job as we did. We started as conductors and got to learn the fare stages and routes, as well as how to handle the passengers, a point which is overlooked in today's situation.

I always tried to put myself in the passenger's seat. How would I feel, if I was going to be late for work because of waiting for a late-running bus; even worse, its raining and there is no bus shelter? You get on the bus (when it arrives) spoiling for a fight and the first person you meet is the conductor, who comes at you, hand outstretched and says one word, "Fare!".

"Alright, give me a chance to sit down!"

"You should have got your money ready while you were waiting" and that was how things started! The conductor is the first person the passenger takes it out on and I've seen many an argument take place, instead of common sense being used.

So, before we became one-man bus drivers, we knew the fares, the routes, how to drive a bus and how to get on (most of the time) with the public. In today's situation, it may surprise you to know, that you can apply to become a bus driver, if you are honest and without any convictions against you; you do not require a driving licence, because the bus company employing you will train you and if you do have a licence, you must have been free of any drink-driving offence. After passing your test, you receive a short period of classroom training, then its onto the road under the direction of another driver. Within a short period, you are out on your own. Should anyone give any thought to becoming a bus driver, in my opinion, it's easier to fly an aeroplane (after training, of course) to New York, than drive a double-deck bus, full of passengers, in the rush hour, from Bournemouth to Christchurch and keep time.

Now that I have more time, I'm 'putting the buses to book' and I hope you enjoy reading my books about the real bus-driving days, as well as the passengers and characters I had the pleasure to work with.

If you have enjoyed reading this book, would you like to send a copy as a gift to a relative or friend?

If your favourite bookshop is unable to oblige, further copies can be obtained from:

Tommy Steele
77 Homelake House
Station Road
Parkstone
Poole
Dorset
BH14 8UD

Price £8.99 plus £1.50 p&p (second class)
Please make cheques/POs payable to T Steele